W9-AOT-589

DRIVING *to* PERFECTION

DRIVING *to* PERFECTION

ACHIEVING BUSINESS EXCELLENCE BY CREATING A VIBRANT CULTURE

BRIAN L. FIELKOW

TWO HARBORS PRESS

Copyright © 2013 by Brian L. Fielkow.

Two Harbors Press
322 First Avenue N, 5th floor
Minneapolis, MN 55401
612.455.2293
www.TwoHarborsPress.com

All rights reserved. No part of this publication may be reproduced, stored in a retrieval
system, or transmitted, in any form or by any means, electronic, mechanical, photocopying,
recording, or otherwise, without the prior written permission of the author.

The advice and strategies contained herein may not be suitable for every situation. This work
is sold with the understanding that the publisher and author are not engaged in rendering
professional services. If professional assistance is required, the services of a competent
professional should be sought.

ISBN-13: 978-1-62652-507-8
LCCN: 2013919523

Distributed by Itasca Books

Book Design by Kristeen Ott

Printed in the United States of America

To my wife, Cheryl, and children, Sydnee, Richard, and Rachel. Thank you for your never-ending love, encouragement, and support.

To my mother, Cookie, and late father, Sidney. Thank you for teaching me how to build a business and a family at the same time.

To the extraordinary employees of Jetco Delivery, Waste Management, The Peltz Group, and Godfrey & Kahn. Thank you for taking the time to help me develop and grow, and for having confidence in me.

CONTENTS

As to methods, there may be a million and then some, but principles are few. The man who grasps principles can successfully select his own methods. The man who tries methods, ignoring principles, is sure to have trouble.

Ralph Waldo Emerson

FOREWORD

This book is perhaps the best I have ever read on how leadership directly drives bottom-line financial results.

In the following pages, Brian Fielkow provides a simple and compelling "flight plan" on how to align and engage people to achieve and sustain organizational excellence. With a career life of nearly forty-five years in diverse senior leadership roles, I have seen many examples of the "good," the "bad" and the "in-between."

My interest in the art and science of leadership started early while serving as a USAF fighter pilot. Since then, I have enjoyed senior roles in both large and small organizations, including executive vice president and chief administrative officer at rail holding company Patriot Rail Corp.; senior vice president at North America's biggest solid waste environmental company, Waste Management, Inc.; vice president and chief safety officer at rail giant CSX; and as the top career safety official at the U.S. Department of Transportation/Federal Railroad Administration.

Whether driving trucks, operating trains, or flying jets, my teams—by definition—have traditionally been asked to perform mission-critical duties without nearby support or supervision. In such circumstances, it is critical that employees truly align and engage around management's vision.

This can be a serious management challenge, but, in this book, Brian shows us how to make that alignment happen based upon his proven formula of success that has dramatically elevated the profitability of his own company.

I first met Brian while we were colleagues at Waste Management in the early 2000s. With our first association, it was apparent that we shared a "kindred spirit" and fervent belief that only by nurturing a culture of employee "ownership" can maximum organizational results be achieved and sustained.

This book is remarkable, convincing, and credible. I have studied at some prominent institutions, including Harvard Business School, under some of the best minds in organizational change and leadership. I have read many books, articles, and essays on the topic. This book is better. Here is why:

- This book isn't theory. It is written with authority by one who has actually "done it" and continues to "do it," versus those who just talk about it.
- Brian directly ties his key principles to hard results with living examples and stories.
- This book shows how to operationalize the key tenants of culture. It shows why a vibrant culture makes a profound difference to the bottom line.
- Brian demonstrates how value-driven leadership is THE competitive advantage in business—even when that business is commodity driven.
- The book contains the perfect mix of "good instincts" and "fact-based" discussions around making a case for change.

- Brian's candidness about his personal lessons from mistakes and miscalculations about the culture is extremely effective. The tone of this book is not self-congratulatory. Rather, it is sincere and humble.
- The chapters on anchoring the culture are extremely effective. I especially focused on branding and the importance of *internal* branding. This is the essence of the mystique that successful companies create.
- One of the most meaningful chapters, to me, is "Operationalizing Your Values." In my experience, this is where many organizations fall flat. This chapter is electric in a book full of magic.
- The simple written affirmation in Chapter 20 is perhaps the best "best practice" I have seen.

I hope you enjoy this book and benefit from its teachings. It will inform, inspire, and compel you to look at your own leadership approach in pursuit of exceptional results.

James T. "Jim" Schultz
Fredericksburg, Texas
May 2013

INTRODUCTION

My father was a successful businessman and a great dad. He made his living owning and operating television, appliance, and furniture retail stores in northeastern Wisconsin. Long before the days of Best Buy and Amazon, retail business was very much conducted locally or regionally.

I loved working in the store selling clock radios, Walkmans and, yes, eight-track tape decks. During those years, I learned the joys and headaches of life as a business owner.

I went to college and law school, always thinking that my career would bring me back to business, hopefully with my dad. One day in the summer of 1988, Dad and I took a drive along a very familiar route near our home. My dad got lost. We laughed it off, but as a precaution, he went to the doctor. The doctor asked him to add six plus seven, and he could not. Three months later, he passed away from a brain tumor at the age of fifty-one.

As my business career progressed, there were many times I wanted to pick up the phone to ask my dad a question. For as much as he taught me, I knew that he had a wealth of experience that I would never have a chance to share as a result of his untimely death.

As a result of my father's early death and my other life experiences, I learned that nothing is forever. We have no guarantees, as a result. I wanted to be sure that my knowledge would be passed on to my children—the desire to share my knowledge with them became the impetus for writing this book.

Even so, I did not start out with the desire to write a book, but rather to create a collection of thoughts and notes I thought I might pass along one day. As my career developed over the last twenty-five years, the volume of notes grew. My journey took me from the practice of corporate law, to becoming COO of a privately held recycling company, to being an executive at a large, publicly traded company, and, finally, to owning my own business.

As my journey continued, it became clear to me that my thoughts centered around a few simple themes. In particular:

- Our time is best spent pursuing excellence while ignoring artificially manufactured goals imposed by third parties.
- The best way to achieve sustained excellence is to focus on creating a healthy company culture. Many companies view creating a healthy culture as a "soft" or "feel-good" exercise, when, in reality, "culture" is a hardcore business proposition. Your culture is your competitive advantage. When it comes to nurturing a vibrant culture, our work is never done. It is an on-going responsibility.
- To successfully build culture, our minds must be in the right place. If we are motivated by fear or paralyzed by past mistakes or shortcomings, we will never be in a position to create an environment of excellence.

- The decision to build a vibrant culture is a strategic choice. It requires effort and energy. It does *not* require a lot of money. Company size or budget must not be a barrier to building a vibrant company culture.

I decided to write this book while I am actively engaged in my own company. Why? Because I can empathize with the struggles, opportunities, and challenges of my readers better than if my perspective was from that of a retired executive or consultant. As such, I am sharing both my successes and my failures with you, knowing that you can adapt these ideas to your own business.

My goal is to share my basic formula with you, and to have you modify it to fit your own situation. At best, this formula is imperfect. I have never "batted one thousand" and would not trust anyone who claims such a track record. With that in mind, I am able to offer you an array of experiences you can readily use in your organization to build or enhance your strong cultural foundation.

Transforming an organization culturally is very much a reflection of your own personal journey as a leader. And, as with any journey, although you may have a destination in mind, at the start you truly have no way of knowing exactly where the journey will end.

Each section of this book is intended to be a step on your own journey. That said, I have neither the desire nor ability to dictate what your journey should look like. Rather, I am simply providing ideas and tools for you to adapt for your own purposes along the way.

I hope you enjoy this book and find it useful as you travel your own path to excellence and drive to perfection!

PART I:

YOUR VISION FOR A VIBRANT CULTURE

1

A Cultural
Moment of Truth

A BUSINESS HAS NO VALUES. Rather, corporate values come from the individuals who work for that business. This is where the role of the leader is fundamental. A value-driven culture must start at the top and migrate through the organization. Most of us are guided by a set of values, but it is often difficult to consistently uphold them, especially when we are distracted by the numerous priorities that face us daily.

We all face moments of truth as we move through our lives. We make every decision in our day based on our values and priorities. But, at some point, we have to decide what is truly important to us. In business, that is the moment of truth.

My awakening to the paramount importance of a value-driven culture came while working as an employee of a publically traded company. My boss was a very headstrong individual. When he locked on to an idea, he would lobby some employees to join his cause and force it upon others until his idea came to fruition. In one crucial scenario, he decided that we should hedge our commodity risk. In our particular circumstance, "hedging" made sense if we held price risk and desired to lock our margin by fixing buy and sell prices. But we had one small problem—we were locking in the sales price of the commodity, but we had no control over our own buying price.

Therefore, there was a legitimate risk that we would buy a commodity on the open market and sell it at a loss due to the hedge contract. To me, this was gambling, not hedging. These transactions made no sense, and a small group of company leaders—which I was a part of—knew it. Our objections fell on deaf ears, however, and we were forced to implement the hedge transaction.

In a value-driven move to counter the hedge transaction, the leadership group I was a member of met to share our extreme concerns. We were faced with two options: 1) lying low to save our high-paying careers; or, 2) choosing to put our careers on the line to expose the dangerous actions being taken by others. By putting our values above everything else, we went to our company's CEO and laid out our concerns. In no uncertain terms, we told the CEO that we would willingly tender our resignations if our boss was allowed to continue down his path, fueled by misguided, misinterpreted, and dangerous business decisions.

Within twenty-four hours, our boss was gone! We had stuck to our values. We had not allowed our fears— including possible job loss—to compromise our desire to do what was right for ourselves and our company. And we had come out ahead.

This lesson has remained with me for the balance of my career. When your moment of truth comes, you will have a very important decision to make. If your personal values are defined—and not negotiable—then your decision will be very easy, even though you may still endure a few sleepless nights along the way.

Prior to that experience, I had a solid set of core values. However, I had never been faced with the possibility of having to put my career at risk for the sake of doing what was right. Every one of us has bills to pay and a lifestyle to support. I learned to separate *priorities* (which might change by the day) from *values* (which are consistent and never compromised). In essence, I had been asked to compromise my integrity (values) for the sake of an ill-conceived and dangerous goal. I chose to put my values first.

Assuming your personal values are defined, then you will be ready to aggressively rise to the challenge of building and leading a value-driven organization. When this happens, it will become clear that your values are non-negotiable. Once your personal values are firmly in place, you will be ready to steer a positive transformation not only in your own career, but also in the life of your organization. And, if your organization's values are tied to your own, you will find that you will not allow your organization to compromise its values any more than you would compromise your own personal values or integrity.

2

Your Vision for a Vibrant Culture

I'VE BEEN FORTUNATE TO HAVE enjoyed a diverse business career. Over the course of the past twenty-two years, I have practiced corporate law and have operated regional and publicly traded recycling companies, and I currently own a growing trucking and logistics company, Jetco Delivery. Throughout my career, I've admired certain companies, often wondering how they consistently outshine their competition. What is their secret ingredient? As I have continued my journey, I've arrived at an undeniable conclusion: their company culture is what sets them apart. While some companies work tirelessly to foster a vibrant, growing culture, many others take it for granted.

Before undertaking the effort to write this book, I had to ask myself what new information I brought to the table. I enjoy reading books by legendary CEOs, and I encourage you to do the same—we need to learn from the best. However, large corporations have access to a depth of resources that companies like mine do not. So, we must adapt their ideas to our organizations. My objective is to help you understand how to bridge that gap with practical, hands-on advice, combined with clear examples that will allow you to achieve cultural excellence no matter the size of your company.

Cultural excellence is the best way to guarantee business success in the face of uncertainty. Of course, *excellence*, *success*, and *uncertainty* are relative terms. I'm not here to tell you what your culture should look like. Rather, my goal is to help you think through what vision will be necessary for you to create your own unique culture that endures uncertainty, breeds excellence, and achieves success. My goal is also to provide you with practical ideas for implementation along the way. Make no mistake: building cultural excellence is a journey—a journey to be led by you.

In its simplest terms, culture is the convergence of people and process. An excellent culture occurs when people and process are in harmony with the company's vision and values. When this happens, employees are empowered and engaged—they share the same beliefs and values as the company and agree with its way of operating. In the best situation, accepted patterns of behavior are clearly expressed and understood, and, ultimately, customers enjoy positive experiences in their interactions with the company.

To prepare for your journey, look around you for signs of cultural excellence in other companies. I like to tell my employees about an extremely satisfying customer experience I had with Apple. My son received a new computer for his birthday. A month later, he dropped it. I took the unit back to the store for service, and the store sent the computer to a service center. A week later, I received a call from a very polite customer service representative (CSR). He said, "Mr. Fielkow, we figured out the problem with your computer. It was dropped." I thought to myself, *No kidding*, and reached for my wallet, expecting a large bill. The CSR then said, "I see you are a good customer and this is a new unit. I am going to warranty it for you. We want you and your son to be customers for life."

In terms of what true empowerment looks like, this was perfection. I did not have to hold for a supervisor, because this employee was empowered to make a decision. On top of that, he was clearly trained to use our specific purchase data to make an assessment about my value as a customer.

As amazing as Apple's technology may be, this act of employee empowerment impressed me far more. Moreover, this story gave me a concrete vision of what excellent customer service looks like so that my own company can understand and emulate it. This is the litmus test by which I measure our service: employees empowered to do what is simply right for the customer.

As you will see throughout this book, I love the small stuff. Excellence lies in the details. If you sit around and wait for a seismic transformation to occur overnight, it may never happen. On the other hand, by capturing and emulating *everyday* excellence, you will begin to create your own mystique. Outsiders will begin to see the difference between your organization and the rest of the pack. And this always starts at the very front lines of your business.

Culture Is:

- Shared beliefs and values
- Empowered employees doing what is right
- Accepted patterns of behavior

- A hard-core business proposition
- Process driven

Above all, culture is a strategic choice.

As we move forward, begin to imagine what an ideal culture looks like to you. Compare it to your status quo. Then, think about how the implementation of an ideal culture would benefit your company.

Envisioning Excellence—It's Always in the Details

When I speak to groups about envisioning an ideal culture, I often use the examples of Apple, Disney, and Ritz-Carlton. I use these examples to demonstrate that even the largest companies are capable of creating excellence at the most detailed level.

Apple: Their excellence is as much about individual empowerment as it is about their amazing technology. I love the above example of a front-line customer service representative who was fully empowered to ensure my satisfaction as a customer—even when I was clearly at fault.

Disney: Their excellence is not about their vast media empire. It's about attention to detail and consistency. Think about Disneyland. Is it ever dirty? Is the experience ever inconsistent? If Mickey Mouse is having a bad day, does he refuse to take a photo with your kids? Next time you go to a Disney theme park, focus on their obsession with every detail to ensure a perfect customer experience.

Ritz-Carlton: If there was ever a commoditized product, it would be hotel rooms. If Ritz-Carlton believed it were simply a provider of hotel rooms, it would be competing on price with the rest of the pack. Ritz-Carlton sells an unparalleled customer experience, led by a fully trained and empowered staff. The brand rises above commoditization because of the service and experience it provides to its guests.

Each of these companies has a secret ingredient that allows it to rise above the rest. As customers, we may take this for granted, but the excellence we experience happens as the result of well-trained people and well-defined processes consistently functioning in harmony.

From the Inside.

After looking outside your business for examples of vibrant cultures, it is critical that you then look *inside* to assess your own. This initial inward review will allow you to compare your own perception of the state of your culture to the perceptions of your employees. Here are a few questions you might want to ask your employees:

1. How would you describe our leadership style?
2. Do you believe that this is a team-based environment?

3. Are you empowered to make decisions? If so, please provide a few examples. If not, why?

In my experience, a vibrant culture will not develop in an autocratic environment where decisions flow from the top down. Employees who are not empowered are simply not engaged in their jobs.

As you digest the answers you have received to the above questions, consider this simple truth:

At its core, your company's culture is behavior based. It is a mix of individual and organizational behavior, all of which is functioning in alignment with your company's values.

If we treat our employees like robots, then we should not be surprised when they behave like robots. If we treat our employees as accountable, empowered professionals, then we should not be surprised when our employees reward us with such behavior. In a traditional, top-down, "command and control" environment, employees lack ownership of their work and do not have a connection to the business. They have no stake in the game, and they will behave accordingly.

Behavior, then, is the foundation of a vibrant culture. As leaders, we should focus a significant amount of our time promoting culturally aligned behavior. Yet, that is not the reality for most of us.

Truthfully, how much time do you spend focused on behavior, either individual or organizational? Instead of driving behavior, do you spend your time focused on what flows from behavior, such as operating metrics, financial data, and safety and compliance statistics?

It is essential that we spend more of our time on the individual and organizational behaviors that drive our outcomes. Many of the ideas in this book will help you promote positive behavior and eliminate counterproductive conduct from your company.

Growth and financial success result from your investment in a behavior-based culture.

Customers are happy and return for repeat business. They recognize something unique about your product or service.

Because employees are empowered and process is in place, products and service are world class.

Leaders invest tremendous effort in building a vibrant, behavior-based culture. As a result, established processes are in place, and employees are empowered.

How much of your time is spent at the base of this pyramid?

3

Rich Culture vs.
Poor Culture

THERE ARE MANY REASONS WHY companies do not take the culture-building plunge. Most often, executives see "culture" as a difficult-to-define, elusive, entity—or a soft-and-fuzzy, feel-good waste of time. I'm here to tell you that measureable business success comes from a company's culture.

Our business culture serves the hardcore business purpose of guiding us as we carry out our mission to achieve excellence and profitability. Culture can be considered a map, as well as the ground rules for what we, as a company—regardless of any individual roles—will not compromise. These values, when clearly articulated and consistently reinforced, will guide all decisions made by anyone in the company—from the front lines to the back offices.

As you embark on this journey, you may encounter resistance and disbelief from those around you. Who can blame employees for their skepticism? Many corporations continuously shift the earth beneath their employees' feet. For many employees, "establishing culture" often equates to the intrusion of outside consultants or catchy one-off themes. But, if implementation is done right, most of the organization should be on board within three to six months—or as soon as you have proven that shared values benefit their roles within the company. Your job is to win your employees over—and to weed out those who cannot be won.

You—as a leader—can create the values that guide your company. Only employees can effectively hold each other accountable for living those values. In other words, you must live your cultural values each day to instill what drives success throughout the organization.

What are the signs of a poor culture? In essence, a poor culture is one in which senior management does not invest in the development of the company and its people or processes. There is neither communication of, nor enforcement of, what are accepted and expected behaviors. Some companies ignore the need for culture building, and others outsource it to outside consultants. In the end, the result of these half-hearted attempts is the same: employees do not adopt a new, vibrant culture because it is not shown to be important to the company's leadership. Basically, the ship is drifting with no captain at the helm.

In a poor culture, everyone works in their silos—their distinct departments or divisions of the company. Employees are more concerned about what is best for themselves or their teams, rather than for the greater benefit of the enterprise. Employees are not empowered and, in fact, are often afraid to make decisions for fear of being wrong. The leaders of a business with a poor culture perform a parental role, simply mediating disputes and being the all-knowing problem solvers.

In a poor culture, new employee orientation happens at the water cooler. Existing employees advise the unfortunate new hires to keep their heads down and mouths shut. New employees are cautioned that innovative thinking is quickly shot down, and that, to survive, you shouldn't make waves.

After I acquired Jetco in 2006, a few employees approached me—coincidentally, by the water cooler. They welcomed me to the company and then gave me some advice: "You take care of us, and we'll take care of you." My new-employee orientation had begun. I knew exactly what my new friends were telling me. If I gave them what they wanted, they would let the rest of the team know that the new owner was okay. On the other hand, if I rocked the boat, things might not work out so well. They obviously wanted a leader who went with the flow, instead of driving new initiatives.

Without a leader advocating for a richer culture, your business culture is being created for you by employees who may not be in line with your values. If you are not investing effort into developing a great culture, I guarantee that your company's culture is being defined for you—at this very moment as you are reading this book.

In a rich culture, senior leadership is fully engaged. However, the culture and its continual development are owned and driven by the employees. Employees instantly know the right action to take because they understand the company's values. They understand the company's process and decision-making framework.

In a healthy culture, the opinion leaders become your greatest asset. Instead of making veiled threats around the water cooler, they are the ones promoting a rich culture. They are educating new employees about the proactive, value-based behavior necessary for success in the company.

Signs that a poor culture is in place:

- Senior management delegates the upkeep of—or ignores—culture and fails to live by the company values
- Culture is seen as a project, not a way of life
- Culture conversations are reactive and occur only when trouble erupts
- Employees lack empowerment and are not appreciated
- Cultural engagement is left to outside consultants and fancy posters with no long-term effort made to make the culture integral to the organization
- Bad behavior is ignored or—even worse—accepted

Signs that a rich culture is in place:

- The whole company is fully engaged in building a world-class culture
- Culture is woven into every "peer to peer" interaction
- Employees share a common vision and are fully empowered to behave in alignment with that vision
- Culture centers around consistent messages which are communicated often throughout the organization
- Silos do not exist
- Customers and outsiders immediately sense a unique experience when dealing with your company because of its culture

The reality is that all businesses are likely to embody elements of both a rich and poor culture. On our path to excellence, we must drive out the poor elements and continuously build upon the rich.

4

Culture and
Competitive Advantage

SHORTLY AFTER LEAVING MY LAW practice
to work for a major recycling firm, I found culture was the
source of extraordinary margins in, of all things, bales of recy-
cled paper and cardboard—the least sexy of all commodities.
We sold our bales to paper mills for thirty percent *more* than
the competitor down the street. Commodity pricing was no
secret, and market prices were published daily for all to see.
Why would anyone pay more than what was published? As it
turned out, paper mills paid top dollar for *reliability*—not for
the commodity itself. Reliability was a core, uncompromising
value of our company. If we promised a certain quality and
quantity of bales in an agreed-upon timeframe, that is what
we delivered. By consistently meeting or exceeding expectations, week after week, our price became less of a factor for
paper mills than the peace of mind that resulted from knowing that their supply lines were secure.

   Ever since I learned why identical bales of cardboard
could sell for such vastly different prices, I have become fasci-

nated with the art of "de-commoditization"—the sale of a commoditized service or product above market price. It is the art of *not* competing on price.

Very few of us sell a product or service that is perceived to be available uniquely from our company. Even so, I have seen many people successfully command a premium price via the "cult of personality." In this scenario where personality is more important than price, a charismatic leader "buys" his customers through vacations, hunting trips, tickets, or other perks. Although this may work in the short term, to create sustainable value—and also successfully de-commoditize your business—I encourage you to focus your entire team on delighting the customer through extraordinary service. This happens when the team lives and breathes the values you bring to the company, in such a way that the customer understands and pays for the unique value this provides.

This happens when you have hired the right people and have implemented the following concepts:

- **Institutionalized service quality.** Once service quality is consistent across the company, quality will not depend on any single employee. From the customer's standpoint, his or her lead contact can go on vacation or leave the company, and high-quality service will continue uninterrupted.
- **Predictable outcomes.** Customer satisfaction goes up when customers do not need to worry about receiving a different quality of service with each order.
- **Employee-owned work.** Your company's culture will become richer once you insist that each employee see his or her work through to completion. There is no passing the buck in a company with a rich culture.

The true test of your process is when things go wrong. I challenge you to follow service failures in your company from beginning to end. When you are trying to find out where things went wrong, here are a few questions to ask yourself:

- Did the customer find out about the service failure from you, or from a third party?
- Did your employees simply fix the problem, or was the fix accompanied by an honest and focused effort to identify the root cause and permanently cure the problem?
- Was the issue swept under the rug and kept within a small silo?
- Or, instead of each of the above, was the issue—along with the root cause—broadly communicated to the entire company in the spirit of crafting a permanent solution?

Watching how your organization responds when things do *not* go right should be a test of your company's cultural strength. Are your employees empowered to successfully resolve problems without excessive managerial involvement?

Let's say you want to sell your company in the future. Sophisticated buyers know that value comes from within the organization. They can sense whether a culture is in place that will survive your departure. This is what drives premium purchase prices for good businesses. Rather than looking solely at financial reports, sophisticated buyers watch how a business runs. They want to know if the operating procedures are understood at all levels of the company. They watch out for people running into the boss's office seeking solutions to their problems. They search for teams of people working across departments to solve problems. They determine if people are empowered to make decisions based on shared values and vision.

Of course, with empowerment comes accountability. If an employee is accountable and empowered to solve a problem, he or she will research it, figure out its cause, and determine what must be done to prevent it from happening again. But, if this person is neither accountable nor empowered, it's likely he or she will pass the buck and the problem will not get fixed, resulting in damage to a customer relationship. As business leaders, we don't have the luxury of letting this happen. Once an employee identifies a problem, that person must continue researching the problem until the root cause is found.

In my business, for example, I am well aware that the industry of moving freight is a highly fragmented industry. There are thousands of companies with trucks, many of whom compete directly with me. However, although there are many freight companies, there is only one Jetco in the world. Why? Because we do not simply sell trucking services. With the help of our experienced employees, we also sell know-how and peace of mind.

My primary role in this process is *not* to "wine and dine" the customer. My role is to ensure that we have the right people and processes in place to ensure a consistent outcome with every customer interaction. This consistency will keep customers coming back with more enthusiasm than they might experience as the result of any night out or any tickets to a ball game. For a thriving cultural difference to saturate your company, it is essential that you invest your time and energy into building something great.

Remember, few of us have the luxury of selling a wholly unique product that cannot be purchased elsewhere. If you believe that your service or product is simply a commodity (as they all are, to varying degrees), you are left to compete on price. And, because buyers are extremely sophisticated, when left unchecked, they will force the company to work for razor-thin margins.

However, if you firmly believe *and demonstrate* that your culture is something no one else possesses and that your unique way of doing things is valuable to the customer, this company culture can become your point of differentiation. Demonstrated clearly, this is your vehicle to grow. After all, if my company could sell an identical bale of cardboard for thirty percent more than the guy next door because of our uncompromising commitment to reliability, there are certainly opportunities within *your* company.

When you look at your own company, how many times have you worried around the clock about the departure of a key employee? Have you ever thought, "If this salesman leaves, how much business will I lose?"

Your culture is your insurance policy, far more so than any non-compete agreement. In a well-functioning culture, the company is bigger than any one person and can withstand the inevitable departure of any key employees. In reality, if you have a strong company culture, your customers will have a bond with the organization, not simply with one individual.

The following are signs of a healthy and vibrant culture:

- Employees are empowered and happy. They see meaning in what they do. As a result, employee turnover is low, and the company benefits from continuity. Customers crave working with empowered employees who deliver more value and solve problems faster. There is recognition that all employees, regardless of status or education, seek a career that is meaningful and challenging. Every person knows that he or she matters.

- There is no fear of retribution. Because a healthy culture promotes continuous learning, employees have no fear of admitting and communicating mistakes. Instead of sweeping errors under the rug, mistakes become learning and growth opportunities for the whole organization.

- Accountability is the norm. An environment where employees are held accountable for themselves creates growth out of setbacks. Conversely, if your company is wired to blame, embarrass, and discipline, you should not be surprised when problems go unaddressed and mysteriously repeat themselves.

- Employees are expected to follow company processes, while also challenging those processes in pursuit of continuous improvement and working to develop new processes without the introduction of unnecessary bureaucracy.

PART II:

ARE YOU PERSONALLY READY TO BEGIN THE JOURNEY?

5

Are Your Fears Leading You?

IN ORDER TO EFFECT POSITIVE cultural change in your organization, the process must start with you. You must be prepared to devote your full focus and energy on creating this new culture. You must be mentally ready to embark on a journey to excellence. This includes getting a firm handle on your own fears and worries.

I, personally, was not mentally ready when my company needed me the most.

The walls came crashing down. At least that's what it felt like. Jetco's business was booming in 2007 and 2008—then the Great Recession hit. The wheels literally came to an immediate halt. People stopped spending. Freight stopped moving. It looked like our very existence was in jeopardy. We had our worst-case scenario plans in place. We followed textbook disaster-planning guidelines. But there was one significant missing piece: I was not mentally ready for the severity of the downturn. Fear took over, and it paralyzed me. Instead of focusing on what needed to be done, I found myself questioning my possibilities. If the business failed, what would it mean to the families who relied on us for a living? What would it mean for my family? What would happen to my sense of self-worth, knowing that my business had failed? I found myself equating the failure of my business to being a personal failure.

One day, at a lunch meeting with two friends, I decided to let it all out. I had internalized all of this anxiety and it was hurting me tremendously, not to mention what it was doing to my company. My friends asked the following simple questions:

1. Since buying the company, it has grown by at least 25% each year. What if sales dropped by 50%?
   My answer: *I know how to run a company with sales that are 50% less than our current run rate, and I enjoy it. We will succeed at that smaller size as long as we make the necessary adjustments.*

2. If the company fails, what would it mean financially?
   My answer: *I have built equity outside of the business. We owe the bank far less than the assets are worth, even in a depressed economy. So, we could liquidate and still come out alive. I know that I could find a meaningful next stage in my career.*

3. If you had to scale back quickly, could you?
   My answer: *Yes. Our main costs are highly variable (people, fuel, insurance). I could collapse my overhead very fast. From there, I could sell assets if needed.*

4. These questions led to the killer question: If business is that bad and at that much risk, why don't you collapse it, skinny back, and ride out the storm?
   My answer to this question was truly an awakening

for me: *We are losing a little money or breaking even. Firing the people that I have worked so hard to grow would set us back years. It would destroy our effort to build something special—a unique culture.*

My fears were killing me. Deep down, however, it was obvious that I knew we could survive and thrive. The faster I could harmonize my paralyzed mental state with my fundamental belief in our ability to succeed, the faster I could position the company for success, even during the Great Recession. Had I not been willing to let my guard down at lunch, fear and uncertainties may have overtaken my business . . . and me.

I realized that I needed to not bottle up my deepest concerns. Talking about my fears allowed me to logically confront them. I realized that my worst-case scenario was not a disaster. I would be fine, and I even had options. Most importantly, this process allowed me to eliminate the illogical and irrational fears that were interfering with my need to effectively lead in a time of crisis.

If you lead from a position of fear, or worry about everything that could go wrong, you will not be able to inspire change. What I went through during the Great Recession may not be identical to what you are facing, but no matter what you are worried about, you need to take care of your own issues, first. Your head must be in the right place before you can be an effective, credible agent of change in your company.

From an early age, we seem to be taught to focus on our fears, failures, and mistakes. Certainly, we cannot ignore problems that must be fixed, but focusing on the negative, "half-empty" mindset can only be a significant barrier to business excellence.

Peer Advisory:
It Doesn't have to be Lonely at the Top!

When deep concerns about your business arise (and they will), where do you turn? Who can you talk to? In privately held businesses, we tend to be vertically organized. Said another way, "It's lonely at the top."

This is especially true at times when you do not want to share possibly overwhelming concerns with your employees. In times of crisis, your employees crave leadership and confidence—and that is what you owe them.

In my experience, a peer advisory group is essential to good leadership. If you don't have co-workers on your level, you need to look outside your own company.

For instance, I have been a member of Vistage International (a professionally facilitated peer-to-peer advisory group) since 1996. Vistage and other groups such as the Young Presidents' Organization (YPO) can perform a vital role in both your business and personal life. Used correctly, a peer advisory group becomes an "outside board of directors" that focuses on your business and, more importantly, focuses on you, personally.

The friends who walked me through my crisis by asking me the above series of questions were fellow Vistage members. And I have helped them through similar situations. Nobody understands your challenges as well as peers who have shared the same experiences.

With a peer advisory group, you have company—not loneliness—at the top!

6

Define Your Role

DEALING WITH YOUR SELF-IMPOSED fears and barriers is essential before you attempt to transform your business. Step back and look at the reality of what you are really doing every day—and what you are avoiding doing. If you are spending all of your time in tactical areas of the business, it is very likely that time which should be spent on vision and direction is being short changed. If you are spending all of your time on strategy and vision, there is a chance that you are missing what is happening on the ground.

Most of our businesses require us to provide strategic leadership and, simultaneously, ensure proper execution of our plans. In other words, we can't focus solely on strategizing, but we also can't spend all of our time on the front lines.

During the early stages of developing my business, I found myself at one extreme. I was too involved in execution, and did not devote enough time to the strategic effort required to build a vibrant culture.

As an example, I used to attend our operation, sales, finance, *and* compliance meetings. If there was a meeting, I was there. Early in our company's life, I attended those meetings because I felt I was the only one able to lead the sessions. In my mind, there was a certain practicality to the situation. As the company evolved, I groomed highly qualified people to lead those areas. Yet, for no obvious reason, I continued to attend the meetings.

In essence, I realized that I had to kick myself out. I found that participants would look to me in these meetings, and, at times, I was inadvertently undermining the leaders I had hired. Now, I work through my leaders and give them space to execute their plans. It is often difficult for us to let go of the "baby" we raised, but it is necessary if we want the company to grow.

And, as my business and culture reached new levels, I learned (sometimes reluctantly) the importance of stepping out of the way to let other talented leaders—whom I had chosen specifically for their talents—perform their jobs. It took some time for me to realize that a business that centers on any one person (or small group of people) is destined to reach its limit—and then stagnate. Moreover, as your company grows and your culture evolves, you simply cannot—and should not—do it all alone. If all problems land on your desk and if all customer visits involve you, the weight of the burden will ultimately crush you. You might experience burnout or, worse, health issues if the stress is left unchecked. As my business grew, I knew my role had to change. If not, I would gravitate toward my comfort zone, and the ship would be adrift!

Because I naturally gravitate to execution-related functions, I had to step back without stepping out. Stepping back allowed me to focus on building our culture, while allowing the people and processes I had developed to ensure proper execution.

As my business changed, I had to change; otherwise, the biggest barrier to sustainable growth would have been staring me in the mirror. I shared my desire to step back with my leadership team, and asked them to hold me accountable.

Don't get me wrong. As we work to help a young business emerge, the answer is clear: we must be involved in all of it. We may not have the resources or depth to think about keeping our hands out of every aspect of the business. The time will come, however, when you have to make the important decision about whether you can hand off critical day-to-day functions so that you can focus on the overall direction of the company. This will mean letting go of sovereignty and building a team that can carry your organization to an entirely new level—a level higher than you could ever achieve on your own.

It will be difficult to transform your company's culture without letting go of the functions that, deep down, you know should be left to other people—most of whom are often better equipped than you are to execute those functions. Executed successfully, this will put you in a position to transform your organization because you'll be able to take the time to see the grand scheme.

Now, assume you simply do not want to let go of the small details. You may enjoy the day-to-day operations of the business more than some of the less tangible, big-picture activities. That is perfectly okay. Each of us has different strengths, and nobody should convince you to lead outside of your zone. But your company still needs someone in that "big picture" capacity.

If you want to drive cultural change but feel you are not the one to do it, look around your company. Do you have a leader (or potential leader) who has the ability and passion to champion this effort?

Building a world-class culture is a strategic decision. It is essential that you have a plan in place for building and anchoring the culture and, as part of that, you should be prepared for your role to evolve along with your business. As your role evolves, look for the balance between strategy creation and tactical execution that matches your style— personal and business success is about balance—and finding the correct fit for you.

As leaders, we must balance strategy and tactical execution. We cannot ignore either.

Strategic Execution	Tactical Execution
Develop, communicate, and promote our values	Manage day-to-day operating metrics
Challenge the status quo and look for new directions	Optimize results from our current infrastructure
Ensure the team knows why we do things a certain way	Direct people to perform a certain way
Ensure each employee understands his or her vital role on the team	Hold people accountable for short-term goals
Set the direction with clarity and purpose	Develop the roadmap to get there
Ensure behaviors are lined up with our values	Focus on production and output

7

Your Value Statement— Your Hedgehog

AS YOU PURSUE EXCELLENCE IN your business, it is imperative that you do a few things well and with focus and clarity. When I have executed poorly, it is invariably because I lost focus on what the organization could reasonably achieve at the time, or I misjudged the opportunity. I was a "fox" when I should have been a "hedgehog."

The story of the fox and hedgehog has been told many times. The story is worth repeating here.

In the original essay "The Hedgehog and the Fox," philosopher Isaiah Berlin divided the world into hedgehogs and foxes, based upon an ancient Greek parable. Berlin pointed out that hedgehogs view the world through the lens of a single, defining idea. Foxes, on the other hand, draw on a variety of ideas, and their world cannot be boiled down to a single unifying concept.

The fox knows many things, but the hedgehog knows one big thing. The fox is a cunning creature, able to devise a myriad of complex strategies for sneak attacks upon the hedgehog. Day in and day out, the fox circles around the hedgehog's den, waiting for the perfect moment to pounce. Fast, sleek, beautiful, fleet of foot, and crafty—the fox looks like the sure winner. The hedgehog, on the other hand, is a dowdier creature, looking like a genetic mix-up between a porcupine and a small armadillo. He waddles along, going about his simple day, searching for lunch and taking care of his home. The fox waits in cunning silence at the juncture in the trail. The hedgehog, minding his own business, wanders right into the path of the fox. "Aha, I've got you now!" thinks the fox. He leaps out, bounding across the ground, lightning fast. The little hedgehog, sensing danger, looks up and thinks, "Here we go again. Will he ever learn?" Rolling up into a perfect little ball, the hedgehog becomes a sphere of sharp spikes, pointing outward in all directions.

The fox, bounding toward his prey, sees the hedge-hog defense and calls off the attack. Retreating back to the forest, the fox begins to calculate a new line of attack. Each day, some version of this battle between the hedgehog and the fox takes place, and despite the greater cunning of the fox, the hedgehog always wins.

It is easy to fall into the same trap the fox falls into. While trying to be everything to every customer, we often forget that someone else—who is focused on only the task at hand—might have more success.

In my business, for example, trucks are ubiquitous. They can be used any time, for any purpose. You name it, we can haul it—cars, perishables, equipment, electronics, etc. And, we can haul it anywhere. A fox would do just that. Instead, however, we only seek business that fits our highly tailored niche. In other words, we have a limited, hedgehog-like scope, which defines the business that we seek.

Our "hedgehog" is actually embodied in our value statement as a constant reminder of the type of business and customers we seek:

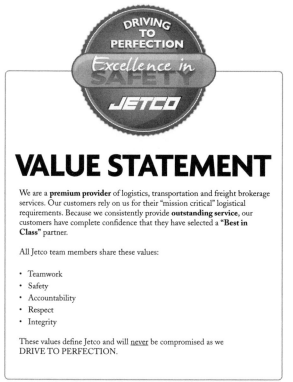

VALUE STATEMENT

We are a **premium provider** of logistics, transportation and freight brokerage services. Our customers rely on us for their "mission critical" logistical requirements. Because we consistently provide **outstanding service**, our customers have complete confidence that they have selected a **"Best in Class"** partner.

All Jetco team members share these values:

- Teamwork
- Safety
- Accountability
- Respect
- Integrity

These values define Jetco and will <u>never</u> be compromised as we DRIVE TO PERFECTION.

Here is how our value statement translated into our hedgehog:

Value Statement Language	Our Hedgehog
Premium provider	We differentiate ourselves based on measurable value. We are not the low-price leader. We are not a fit for purely price-driven customers.
Best in class partner	We operate on a relationship-based model. Our customers know us. We know them. We seek to cultivate prospects with this potential. We do not look for "spot" business.
Outstanding service	If we cannot do the job well, we will not do the work. If the work fits into our core competencies, we will be the best. I would rather pass up a job than execute it poorly.

Our challenge is to stay true to our hedgehog, while at the same time remaining open to change. The right kind of change may cause healthy growing pains as the company entrepreneurially expands. In comparison, unfocused change and idea overload cause the company to dart from one thing to the next without clarity, focus or reason.

Define your hedgehog, build it into your value statement and ensure that your whole team understands it. When presented with an opportunity that is outside the hedgehog, either (a) make a conscious decision to expand the hedgehog; or, (b) just say "no."

The fox and the hedgehog concept must also apply to you as a leader, and not just your company. I see so many executives who dart from one activity to the next with no purpose or cohesion. They are careful with every penny, but waste *time* as if it were an unlimited resource.

I have worked with leaders whose actions and values changed by the day. They were all foxes. Their teams were frustrated because each day was a new and unpredictable venture into the wilderness.

It is important that each one of us defines his or her own personal hedgehog so that we can focus on matters of paramount importance to us. I have worked with some extraordinary business people. Each was a hedgehog. They knew their values and purposes, and their teams knew the same. Although their priorities changed with the demands of the business, their core principles were immutable.

Remember: A business cannot succeed like a hedgehog if its leadership team is a bunch of foxes!

8

Be Ready for Setbacks

AS YOU BEGIN THE PROCESS of transforming your company, the setbacks will come. No one will take more joy in reminding you of the setbacks than the naysayers. Those internal and external constituents who oppose your efforts to transform your business will delight at the first chance to affirm that the previous status quo was acceptable. In addition, self-doubts will certainly arise. You'll no doubt find yourself asking, "Did I take the correct action? Is there a payback for all of the time and energy that I am investing?"

As I look back at the beginning of my journey, I wish that someone would have offered this advice to me: *No matter how well you execute your business and no matter what you do, one or more initiatives will fail. They may fail spectacularly. On top of that, some people will resist change at all costs and drain your positive energy. So, prepare for it now. This is the reality. Get used to it.*

If you are unwilling, or unable, to demonstrate the resiliency needed to meaningfully transform your company, then stop right now. If every challenge or failure plagues you with paralyzing self-doubt, then you may need to re-think your overall direction—or determine if you have the fortitude to lead this all-consuming initiative. Normal concerns and course corrections are healthy and expected. I am talking, here, about doubts that go to the very core of your ability to lead.

Our "Driving to Perfection" culture, for instance, was designed to foster accountability. In the trucking business, our employees are on the road alone and, usually, unsupervised. The only way to ensure service and safety excellence is to ensure that our employees internalize our culture and values and know the right actions to take without being told.

When we started out, some stakeholders thought that trusting our employees to uphold our culture and values was a nice—but impractical—idea. They felt that our truck drivers needed rules and regulations, not a cultural undertaking. Because I believed so firmly in the principle that all people have the same basic human needs, I knew this to be false. I was certain that a value-driven culture was the only way to ensure long-term success.

Then, the setbacks came. After all of our effort, we still had accidents. We still had needless employee turnover. We still had service failures. And, with each instance, I was advised that it would make more sense to fix the problem at hand (in other words to simply "clean up the mess") than to invest in the culture.

To be completely honest, as a result of certain significant setbacks, I was tempted to stop my efforts to transform the business into something greater. However, I stayed with my convictions, and, over time, results improved and we took the company to higher levels in terms of growth and profitability. We still have our share of issues. However, that said, if you ask any of our long-term employees or customers to compare our company now to our company five years ago, you will receive the same answer: the positive difference is significant and measurable.

I am fully aware that resistance to any change or forward motion is encountered almost universally, and this resistance can wear you down. As an example, I recently made a presentation to a group of executives in Portland, Oregon. I received this feedback from my host:

> Without exception, all enjoyed and were "moved" by what you've accomplished and what you had to say. Every comment was positive! However . . . some of what I heard from those that apparently didn't "get it," revolved around comments such as "I've tried that . . . [my employees] won't do it," or "I can't get my people involved in something like that the way his people did." The best one (and I only heard these three) was "My people are cynics, it'll never fly." Hence, my comment about not getting the "top down" aspect of a challenge like this. What those three people obviously missed was the idea that "traction cannot be obtained without 'the boss' pulling just as hard (or harder than), or struggling just as much with the concept as (more than) his/her staff. While, at the same time, being aware enough to be able to see things start to slip, recreate the wheel, keeping it fresh, new."

> What was apparent in those comments was
> that there are those, regardless the level of
> "success" achieved, who believe it sufficient
> to tell others what to do . . . and then, there
> are those who are an actual example of what
> to do.
>
> Keep it up!!

This feedback did not surprise me. While most people are open to change and new ideas (even if they are appropriately skeptical), some will resist change. The business world is full of naysayers—people who will protect the status quo at all costs. It is essential, as we drive change, that we rise above the cynics. If we let them win, they will drain our energy and eventually cause us to lose confidence in the positive steps we are taking on the journey toward building a world-class company.

No matter what changes you desire to make—or objectives you seek to achieve—you will encounter obstacles. Part of being ready to lead a transformation is preparing for this at the beginning of the journey. Do not wait for a setback to hit before dealing with it. This will help you to be ready to lead your organization to a new level of excellence.

While you're thinking about setbacks, ask yourself: "What does my Plan B look like? What contingency plans do I have in place when (not if) the inevitable obstacles are in my way? How am I going to deal with the naysayers in my organization?"

Inviting Setbacks

While setbacks and failures are an inevitable part of running a business, we often needlessly invite them. They are more likely to occur when we let our guard down, so if the following attitudes or behaviors are part of your culture, watch out!

- Complacency
- Cockiness
- "We are doing well. Why push to do better?"

Once you have successfully climbed the mountain, celebrate the success . . . briefly. Realize that you are not done, and that the journey is just beginning. If the celebration lasts too long and you let your guard down, you're bound to run into avoidable setbacks waiting just around the next corner.

PART III:

IDEAS FOR
GETTING STARTED

9

Never Waste a Good Crisis

IN CHAPTER 5, I DISCUSSED how we must manage our own fears and apprehensions before tackling the problems we face in our businesses. Once we are mentally ready for the battle, bring it on!

In 2010, Jetco received the Vistage International Leadership Award for judgment. Normally, I do not like to brag about awards, but this one was special. Vistage (as mentioned above) is an international organization consisting of peer advisory groups and resources serving business executives. There are 16,000 members spread over fifteen countries.

Even with such a broad base, Vistage recognized *our* company for the judgment we displayed during the Great Recession. What did we do? We developed a plan to grow our way through the downturn. Here are the specifics:

Employees first: Just as I had to deal with my own fears, I needed to be empathetic. All of our employees faced the same (and worse) struggles I was facing. Our employees' friends, relatives, and neighbors were being laid off *en masse*.

We recognized this and held frequent meetings to discuss our plan to thrive. In particular, we promised no layoffs unless conditions deteriorated significantly. We explained to our employees that we had decided to sacrifice immediate profit in return for a greater long-term benefit. In return, we asked for extra effort from our employees to help us grow the business. We replaced fear with hope, challenge, and optimism. Nobody left the office afraid of a layoff. Moreover, we built tremendous goodwill and loyalty within our staff.

Seize the abundant opportunity: We sought to capitalize on the realities of the broader market. We hired excellent employees who had been laid off by their previous employers. We bought equipment at bargain-basement prices. We saw other companies' struggles as an opportunity to add to our own pool of talent and assets.

Redefine customer relationships: Our customers were reducing staff and forcing their remaining employees to do more with fewer people. We recognized this challenge and employed technology to create a greater link between our customers and us. We moved to paperless invoicing and automated project status updates, and started placing our own personnel on site at customer projects. These initiatives succeeded in creating perceived value that went well beyond our historic core capacities.

Stakeholder communication: We were transparent with our lenders and other stakeholders. We communicated our plan and provided frequent updates. They knew to expect diminished profits in the short run. Our bank became our partner in the process. Because of this, we never had to worry about our line of credit, and we always had access to capital to purchase assets at distressed prices.

During times of crisis, people are more willing to listen—and change. As leaders, during times of stress, we are given more latitude to put our organizations in place for a better tomorrow. Because of those things, I say to "never waste a good crisis." Instead, use it as an opportunity to transform your organization.

Vistage International recognized that we did not waste the crisis caused by the Great Recession, but, instead, executed a plan to capitalize on the crisis. And, because of how well we did, we received the award I mentioned earlier.

If you have a crisis on your hands, view it as an opportunity to aggressively drive change. Because people view their livelihoods as dependent on the company's survival, you will never have a more willing audience.

Of course, while you should never waste a good crisis, please do not manufacture one either. We have all worked with leaders who seem to develop a new crisis each week. Employees will eventually see right through this manipulative behavior and become desensitized. So, when a real crisis hits, no one will embrace it or rise to the occasion.

10

The Facts Don't Lie!

WITHIN MY COMPANY, WE DID not waste that "good" crisis. Everyone knew that the crisis caused by the economic crash was undisputed—no one could argue that point. In reality, most crises are not as obvious to everyone outside—or even inside—a company, and there is often a disagreement as to whether a crisis even exists at all.

For example, my company experienced a downturn in safety performance. Unlike the crisis imposed by the Great Recession, not everyone in the company perceived that a crisis was at hand. Some viewed our safety issues as a few bumps in the road, better dealt with at an individual level. In contrast, I saw our safety challenges as an opportunity to elevate the organization to a new level of excellence.

I knew it would be easier to transform our culture if my team agreed that the downturn in safety performance was, in fact, a crisis. We were managing off individual perceptions where some people perceived a crisis and others did not. To overcome this standstill, we needed hard-core facts.

To obtain the essential safety facts, we gathered data by conducting individual employee interviews designed to help us to understand and diagnose *employee* perception of the state of our culture. I knew that data would solidify the case for change and address any incorrect perceptions. Without this data, it would have been much more difficult to articulate a defined and credible case for change.

When determining the magnitude of a possible crisis, the questions you should ask depend on the problem(s) you seek to diagnose. To provide you with a taste of what we asked, here are a few examples:

Review the following four focus areas. Rank them by the priority you personally give to them, with "1" being the most important to you.

_____ *Customer Service*
_____ *Safety/People*
_____ *Productivity/Efficiency*
_____ *Cost Control/Financial Interests*

Review the following four focus areas. Rank them by the priority you think your boss would assign to the same items ("1" is more important to your boss/senior.)

_____ *Customer Service*
_____ *Safety/People*
_____ *Productivity/Efficiency*
_____ *Cost Control/Financial Interests*

> *Does Jetco have goals/a vision that are known at all levels of the organization? What is the company's vision as you understand it?*
>
> *How would you describe the culture at Jetco? What are the first things you would do to improve the culture at Jetco if you were in charge?*

I have shared these questions with you to give you an idea of what we wanted to learn. I was testing for shared valued and alignment. You will want to tailor questions like these to meet your objectives, focusing on whatever issue you have on hand. To ensure that you have adequate data that will help you better understand the current state of affairs, ask open-ended questions and conduct the surveys in person. The best answers will come out of a conversation, not a simple "Yes/No" survey.

Through the survey process, we found answers like these:

- "Upper management may know the vision, but I do not. I just work here."
- "We have values. But, when the heat is on, the values are out the window."
- "Nobody takes the time to understand or ask for our input."
- "Working here is about being told to do something . . . or else. It is abrasive."

And the list went on.

From this input, we drew some general conclusions about our status quo:

- The passion for our values varied by department. Passion, in general, was not shared company-wide.
- There was no common vision, or "Jetco way," of doing things.
- Our management staff carried a baseball bat to attack problems, when, instead, our team often needed coaching.
- Our messages were not consistent, and there was a gap between what was preached and what was practiced.

Game over! The data did not lie. There could be no argument about the need for change.

However, we had to face the fact that the negative visible incidents were not the root cause of the problem. The root cause was a culture that was not functioning at its peak level, and behaviors that undermined excellence.

As you seek to transform your own business, start with a diagnostic process. The data will point your team to the most pressing issues—and they may not be what you're expecting. Without this data, needless time will be wasted arguing about whose perception is more accurate. In other words, with data you can focus your efforts on the real issues, and not waste your time shooting blindly at every potential problem.

Breaking the Ice

For me, the most difficult part of undertaking a new and uncomfortable initiative is the beginning. I am always concerned about making sure that the team understands the mission, as well as my ability to properly scope out the purpose of the initiative.

I tried the following idea when employee turnover had become an issue at my company. I scheduled a Saturday meeting with a diverse cross section of our employees to tackle the problem.

To make sure that everyone (including me) came to the meeting focused and prepared, a week before the meeting I sent out this message:

Team, this Saturday we are coming together to review the topic of employee engagement and retention. We must be world-class in this area, and we are not.

To help in planning our meeting, please answer the following question: "If I were a CEO for a day and could take one action for our company to become world-class in the area of employee engagement and retention, I would do the following: _____
_____."

This exercise was beneficial on many levels:

- It broke the ice before the meeting began. Participants knew the issues and were already thinking about them.
- It confirmed in my mind that the answers were already "in house." My job was to draw them out.
- It created a mental picture in everyone's mind—"If I were CEO, I would have the power to . . . ." This opened the door for me to reinforce to my team that no matter your title, you have the power to create change. In essence, I was telling them that they were all CEOs over the destiny of this company.

Before you engage in a new and unfamiliar process, consider how to create a comfortable launch. By breaking the ice, you will gain faster momentum and promote more immediate buy-ins among your stakeholders.

11

Communicating the Case for Change

NOW YOU HAVE A BURNING desire to bring your company to a new level—to transform the culture—and you have the data to support the case for change. But how and where do you begin?

Take, for example, my recent meeting with an executive who transitioned from a large public company to a small up-and-comer with tons of potential. The list of challenges in taking his new, small company to the next level was long. When the conversation turned to examining the culture of the organization, his barriers went up.

"Only the big guys are doing culture stuff," he said. "We don't have the budget. We are too small to concern ourselves with building a culture. I don't have the time."

Mental barriers like these must be removed for all of us. Small stature won't kill you, but small *thinking* will lead to the demise of what you are out to accomplish. You don't need large budgets and high-paid consultants to create an enduring culture. Regardless of the size of your company, either you can create the culture, or others will create the culture for you. "Lack of time" is merely an excuse.

After the data-gathering process, we took the plunge by hosting a company-wide meeting. The goal of the meeting was to promote staff alignment around the vision for a brighter future through a greatly improved company culture.

The meeting involved the following:

- A call to action—we reviewed our current situation with our team with complete transparency. There was no sugar-coating of the data we had found during the assessment process.
- A poll based on the question "What does a world-class culture look like?" We allowed people to dream—to envision what it would be like to work in a world-class environment that was grounded in defined and uncompromising values.
- Finally, we asked "How do we get there?" This was the key to the meeting. In small groups, our employees helped us to answer the following:
  o What is the ideal vision for our culture?
  o What are the obstacles we will encounter?
  o What are the action steps?
  o How will the company look six months from now?

From this series of questions, some common themes emerged. Our employees provided us with the roadmap to transform our company, and, in the process, became stakeholders in the outcome. For the sake of simplicity, I broke up the feedback into "Keep it Up" (what are we doing well now?) and "Please Stop" (what do we need to change?). Here are some examples:

- Keep it Up
  - o Open-door policy
  - o Bonuses
  - o Honest commitment to culture
  - o Equality: You treat us with respect
  - o "Time out" rule: When in doubt, call a timeout
- Please Stop
  - o Address complaints faster. This will improve morale. Don't ignore morale issues!
  - o We hear about changes second hand, or after the fact. Need better all-around communication.
  - o Too quick to play the "blame game."
  - o Too many people are involved in one thing. Define the chain of command and communicate it.

Out of this kick-off meeting came alignment around the following items:

- Trust and understanding
- Agreement around what must change
- The commitment to our core values

Ground Rules for a Fierce Conversation:

As you begin the process of culture change, you should expect passionate, highly charged conversation. To keep the meetings under control, I suggest that you establish a code of conduct. Here is what has worked for me:

- Be tough on the issues and gentle on the people
- Participants may not place blame or make excuses without offering a clear solution
- Stick to the agenda, with new topics added only with group consent
- What is said in the room remains confidential
- Each attendee is expected to speak his or her mind—there are no negative consequences resulting from expressing honest thoughts
- Everyone is accountable for complying with all deadlines agreed to at the meeting

Had this meeting been a one-time special event, the results would have been negligible. However, we made a promise that this meeting was only the beginning of a renewed journey to excellence.

I encourage you to think about the crucial matters in your company which are most important to you. Then, consider a simple set of steps you can use to focus your team around your vision. At that point, you will be in the position to drive change.

When managers seek to drive change in our company, they might call a meeting. Maybe it will include the team at top. Maybe it will include one or two levels below. What is missing? The front lines of the company—the production workers, the customer service representatives, the warehouse staff, or the truck drivers. Your front-line employees are often nowhere to be found in planning meetings. Management takes the two-day retreat and leaves them behind. Yet, in many cases, the people on the front lines know better than anyone what is causing the problems that our organizations are facing. Moreover, if they are included, they can be the leading advocates of change.

We wrongly exclude our front-line employees because of the mistaken assumption that we are smarter than our front lines and that our job is to "enlighten" them. That thinking—which has been around for centuries—is obsolete. A well-functioning company should not be a hierarchy. Rather, it should be a holistic team, consisting of work groups aiming for a common goal.

What I have learned over the past twenty-five years is simple: Regardless of our education, position, or title, we are all human beings, first and foremost. From the person starting at minimum wage to the most highly compensated executive, we all have the same basic needs—to be included, respected, and appreciated. By being inclusive as you transform your company, you will create a tremendous internal base of support. Moreover, you will benefit from the abundant (and often overlooked) wisdom in your company.

12

Creating Organizational Accountability

COMING OUT OF OUR COMPANY-wide meeting, we realized that our environment had to change. For employees to engage in culture-building, management must first create an environment where employees trust that their ideas and participation will not result in retribution. Company meetings must be interactive listening sessions, not lectures. There must be ground rules (as we discussed in Chapter 11) to ensure you attack the problem and not each other. Everyone must be reminded that the premise behind these meetings is the greater good of the company and, by association, its employees.

When cultivating a value-driven culture, all levels of the company must be held accountable to operate and behave within the established norms. Accountability is fundamental to building and sustaining a vibrant organizational culture. Without a culture of accountability, it is impossible to learn from our mistakes and continuously improve. As we begin the journey to create a vibrant company culture, we must remember that employees cannot be held accountable if the organization itself does not behave with accountability.

The difference between individual and organizational accountability is often overlooked, but the difference is profound. Individual accountability flows from the acts or omissions of an individual. For example, take an employee who is properly trained and educated on a given process but unilaterally fails to adhere to that process. The employee may improvise in contravention of the policy, causing something to backfire. In contrast, organizational accountability stems from an act or omission committed by your company—which usually impacts the company as a whole.

Often, when something goes wrong, we perform a root-cause investigation. We ask questions such as:

- *What happened?*
- *What malfunctioned?*
- *Who was most closely associated with the negative outcome?*

These questions lead us to the machine that failed or to the front-line employee who was most closely associated with the outcome. Maybe the inquiry will lead us to his or her supervisor. However, it will often not lead us to the underlying systemic process or failure that went wrong at an *organizational* level.

Take, for example, our drivers at Jetco who are responsible for securing their cargo. This action is essential to prevent damage and accidents. We asked ten of our drivers the best way to secure a certain type of cargo, and we received ten different answers. It was clear that there was not a single, published and digestible best practice in place. There was not a "Jetco Way" of handling this particular type of cargo. Now, let's say that a driver used his/her best judgment, but an accident occurred. While the driver would still have been individually accountable, the organization would also need to look in the mirror to determine the larger cause of the accident. Part of the root-cause review would surely be that we did not have a well-communicated best practice for that procedure.

Examine your company. Consider something that may have gone wrong or an area that could be improved. Review the circumstances and ask whether they resulted purely from an individual's failure or from a flaw in the company's process. These questions should help you probe for organizational accountability:

- *Were roles and responsibilities clearly defined?*
- *Was there proper planning, monitoring and communication prior to execution?*
- *Were the employees trained? Was the training clear and documented?*
- *Were all levels of the company behaving in alignment with the process or objectives?*

Your answer to these questions will allow you to determine whether the challenge relates to one employee—acting on his own—who went astray, or whether there is a deeper issue inside your company. After all, how can we expect our employees to stand up and be accountable if our organization fails to do the same?

Organizational Accountability	
Individual Accountability	Organizational Accountability
• Individual employee fails to follow process; cuts corners • Machine/piece of equipment fails due to operator error • Customer service representative ignores details and enters wrong data	• Company's operating procedures are not understood • Process is not taught or communicated • Audit and review program does not exist or is insufficient • No institutional memory — company makes the same mistake over and over • A preventative culture is not in place to promote and enforce acceptable behaviors

If respect and accountability are core values of your company, how do you treat employees who come forward after making a mistake? Is the employee scolded or thanked for coming forward?

Take the example of the near-miss incident. Each of our companies has experienced a near-miss—likely several of them. In the safety world, a near-miss is the accident that did not happen. Think of two planes that almost collided in mid-air. Near-miss incidents come in all shapes and sizes:

- The critical production deadline that was almost missed
- The overlooked detail that might have caused erroneous financial reporting
- The wrong shipment that was caught just prior to pick up

It is painfully difficult to capture near-misses. The reason is simple: if managers blame employees for the near-misses, then employees will have a disincentive to report them. This means that managers will know less about what is really going on, and the number of near-miss occurrences will only grow. If a root cause cannot be identified, fixing the problem becomes increasingly difficult. Ultimately, the near-miss turns into a serious incident. If you dig deep enough, you will often find that the flaw lies somewhere inside the company and not with a single, wayward employee.

In a positive culture, employees are empowered and encouraged to report signs of trouble. If the problems are out in the open, then the root causes can be attacked and eliminated. As leaders, it is our job to praise those who spot and report trouble, thereby fostering an environment that is receptive to change. In essence, this is how we build organizational accountability.

Once you have created a culture of accountability and empowerment, your employees will not be afraid to come forward. They will become your company's champions of change. They will know that recognition, not retribution, is the result of protecting the organization. This environment ensures that you have a culture in place that embraces and promotes change.

In order to create an environment that welcomes cultural change, try these ideas:

- **Abandon command and control.** Management's role moves from controlling the outcome to empowering the team to create and implement the change.
- **Open the doors of communication.** Make it OK for an employee—or for the organization—to admit a failure, accept accountability and commit to improving. There can be no fear of retribution.
- **Understand and eliminate the threats.** Don't leave

your employees wondering "Will the change result in the loss of my job or someone being promoted above me?" If these questions are not being asked overtly, they are lying below the surface. Anticipate and address your employees' fears directly.

- **Clearly set forth the case for change.** People should not be expected to embrace what they do not understand.
- **Set milestones for deliverables.** Most people have no patience for an initiative that could take years to bear fruit. Even if the goal is time consuming and long term, ensure that the team can enjoy many tangible milestones along the way.

The Answer Is Not In the Handbook.

Traditionally drafted handbooks, rules and regulations are overrated.

While legally necessary, many of us invest a fortune in handbooks and standard operating procedures that, if we are lucky, five percent of our people read and even fewer will absorb the material. The real training and development occurs when teams work together and are guided by shared values.

It's about sharing what happened—and why. It's about holding each other accountable for continuous improvement.

As this is happening, ask your employees to document a day in their life. This will become the basis for a more powerful handbook which is drafted and owned by the very people who are responsible for following it.

13

Driving Change from the Top

AS YOU PREPARE TO TRANSFORM your company's culture, some team members may resist or refuse to see the value in all the effort. In my situation, I came to the conclusion that the status quo was not acceptable and that we had to change. This was a unilateral decision, but the journey would have been fruitless had the rest of my team not joined the effort. Even so, there are times when you must force change because it is the right thing to do. Sometimes, this means taking a calculated risk.

For example, in 2008, I made a value-based decision that could have caused us to lose a substantial portion of our drivers. But, in my business, "no drivers" means no revenue!

In our industry, drivers are only allowed to drive and work a limited number of hours per day and per week. Drivers are required to log their hours to ensure compliance with the law. While most companies take this requirement seriously, a meaningful minority do not. And, at the same time, drivers can find many creative ways to falsify their logs in order to work more than they are legally allowed.

In 2008, GPS technology had evolved to the point where it made log falsification all but impossible. I made a unilateral decision that we were putting GPS tracking systems in all of our trucks. My team had input on the details, such as vendor selection, but my decision was not negotiable. When word spread, you can imagine the uproar. I heard every objection in the book:

- I don't like technology.
- Big brother is watching—don't you trust me?
- This is going to cost me work hours and money.

I understood these objections, but my decision was non-negotiable. In my mind, if safety and integrity were two of my company's core values, this change was essential and obvious. I could only think of the possibility of a fatigued driver working over his or her legal limits and killing someone. I was determined that this would not happen on my watch!

Several quality drivers threatened to quit if we executed our plan. In reality, only one driver quit, and he ended up coming back. GPS did not cost anyone a cent in lost wages, and—as an added and unexpected bonus—the technology helped us eliminate a lot of bureaucracy and paperwork for those employees in the office *and* those on the road. Over time, our team of drivers came to appreciate that the use of the GPS technology was as much for their protection as it was for the company's.

My decision was value based, plain and simple. It was completely based in how I choose to live my business life. So, how did I bridge the seemingly enormous gap between my decision to operationalize our values and the potential consequences?

Empathy: We anticipated and understood the possible concerns. Major change is frightening for many employees, so we acknowledged the legitimacy of the worry. Being empathetic was a way to let my team know that we were not deaf to their concerns.

Over Communication: We selected a handful of employees to be on our beta team—including some of the most vocal opponents to the change. We kept this axiom in mind: *Those who participate are likely to support. Those who are excluded are likely to oppose.* We built supporters by bringing them inside.

As our beta team became comfortable with the process change, they spread the word. They addressed our team's fears in ways that had greater credibility than I could ever garner.

Five years later, this transformation is part of our DNA. It has been a success in every respect. I made a unilateral, non-negotiable decision, and it turned out to be the right one. More importantly, I recognized that the battle would be won or lost in how we *implemented* the change—not in the change, itself.

As a leader, you must stand up for what you believe is right, and some decisions will not be up for discussion. However, by being empathic while carefully defining an implementation process around the change that you desire to create, you can convert opponents to allies. And, if your vision was correct, the team will come to support and respect it.

14

Communicating a Higher Purpose

AS WE RUN OUR COMPANIES, we become consumed by the day-to-day demands of the business, and forget about the people who help us succeed. Our employees know what to do, but do they know why they matter? You cannot use rewards or penalties to instill culture or passion in an employee.

Instead, invest your effort in creating a sense of purpose. At the core, do your employees know how much they matter as human beings? Do they understand how important they are to you and your customers? I love using this photo to illustrate the point:

This photo is of a truck accepting cargo from an international port. My employees could see themselves as "just truck drivers" or "just dispatchers" or "just customer service representatives." The above photo offers a completely different perspective. Specifically, it illustrates that, without drivers, dispatchers, and customer service representatives, the freight does not leave the ship. In fact, without each of them, nothing moves: hospitals do not have their life-saving equipment, garbage piles up, retail shelves are bare. After all, everything you own was, at one point, transported on a truck.

Who do you suppose comes to work with passion and motivation—"just an employee" or the professional who understands his or her vital role in the important contribution that your business makes to society?

Look again at the above photograph. What would your "big picture" image look like? What is it about your company that employees can rally around so that a shared understanding of purpose exists?

Let's say that your company services air conditioners. Envision a family with an ill, homebound child. Your technician must view herself as having to perform to the highest possible standard. If her work quality is anything less, let her imagine the discomfort that child will experience on a sweltering summer day. The mindset of someone offering critically important aid to a child is a very different mindset from that of a person who "just fixes air conditioners."

You—as the person driving your company's culture—have the unique ability to instill a higher purpose in your employees.

15

Winning Employees to Your Culture

AS YOU DEFINE YOUR CULTURE and begin the process of change, be prepared to win some employees and lose others. At a previous company, I hired two highly talented employees. Both had started at my company at about the same time and brought a wealth of energy, ideas, and enthusiasm to the organization. I had big plans for each of them. Unfortunately, both were out of line with our culture.

Brett was egocentric, believing that the organization revolved around him. He failed to recognize that he had joined a successful company which was built on a history of success. He chose to believe that our company had been drifting without direction until he arrived to save us. On the other hand, Brenda belittled her co-workers and would channel customer compliments into "I won, you lost" conversations with her peers.

Clearly, they both posed problems for me to deal with. We enjoyed the services of both Brett and Brenda. They both were productive, but their co-workers were unhappy. We coached both employees, using a variety of techniques. Supervisors, managers from other departments, and co-workers all worked with Brett and Brenda. We held them accountable for their actions and offered clear, written feedback. In the end, Brett changed, but Brenda did not. Let me be clear— Brett did not change overnight. We spent at least six months on the process. Brett occasionally slipped back into his old ways and we needed to help him get back on track. That said, however, he became one of our best-performing employees and one of our cultural ambassadors.

Unfortunately, we had to let Brenda go. With her skills, I am sure she was able to thrive in another company— just not ours. We made the decision that our values and culture are not negotiable. We have made it clear that it is not the employee's choice to accept or reject our culture. Instead, our culture will ultimately weed out those who choose to follow a different path. Had we failed to make a sincere effort to coach both Brett and Brenda, we might have lost both of them. The process of coaching to promote cultural alignment can pay tremendous dividends, and having Brett as part of our company continues to do so to this day.

As you embark on building your own culture, be aware that when you begin the process, you will find that some of your best performers won't share the company's values. With this in mind, know that the majority of employees will expect you to protect the culture—even if it means firing the good performers who are out of line with the culture. Of course, to truly show your commitment to a stronger culture, you will want to coach any employee from multiple levels prior to firing them, by involving executives, managers, and even peers. But, if it doesn't work, you will need to transition them out.

As executives, we are slow to dismiss those who are out of line with our culture. After all, if we have twenty other things that are clearly broken—and these types of people are performing well and appear unbroken—it is hard to make them a top priority. But when a cancer is present, it will grow within your organization. People in line with the company's culture who are performing well will begin to wonder why they are held accountable and "the cancer" is not. You must be prepared to remove these employees while rewarding exemplary, culturally aligned behavior.

If you design your company around shared values tied to clear economic and business benefits—and you promote and encourage those values throughout your organization—you will see across-the-board improvement over time. Excellence requires the pursuit of perfection and nothing less. In the immortal words of Vince Lombardi, "Perfection is not attainable, but if we chase perfection, we can catch excellence."

Signs of Contamination in Your Environment

As leaders, it is our duty to continually monitor the workplace for employees who contaminate the environment. These employees will destroy the morale of the greater team. Moreover, if we fail to take action, we are risking our credibility among the majority of employees who work hard to promote a healthy culture.

Here are a few signs of potential contamination in your culture:

- The leader looks the other way if bad behavior stems from an otherwise productive or specially-skilled employee.
- An employee who has a social relationship with the boss receives preferential treatment.
- The leader preaches value and culturally-aligned behavior, but his actions are contrary.
- The leader has a group of favorite employees. These employees live by a separate set of rules. They advance quickly and always seem to be on the inside track regarding company developments or progress.
- Small cliques form in the office. These cliques become the catalyst for negative behavior. As they gain strength, the cliques bully otherwise satisfied, productive employees into an anti-company mindset.

We often celebrate *results*. As we build a vibrant culture, we must also celebrate *behaviors*. Winning employees over to a culture of excellence is about celebrating behaviors driven by shared values. Once your cultural values are established, seek out and celebrate those who are living your culture. Look for an employee who resolves a customer concern without escalating the issue to an unnecessary level of management. Find an employee who makes a judgment call that saves lives. Highlight an employee who works across departments to create value for a customer. Regardless of whether a success is large or small, celebrate it along the way.

If establishing cultural values within your organization is a new concept, there will be a need for some formal training, teaching, and company-wide alignment with the values you create. Culture and values are defined at the top, but they are not handed down and left to fester. For a positive culture to spread throughout the organization, employees must be encouraged and reminded every day that values lead to excellence, which is followed by success.

Above all, you will want to ensure that everyone within the organization knows what you are doing and why you are doing it. Perhaps your company is experiencing some negative trends that must be addressed. Maybe you want to take the company to a new level of success. Or, it could be that the owner is retiring and changes must occur for the company to survive. Whatever you decide is your reason for moving forward, this should be your rallying cry—and can be achieved through getting employees to work with you to transform your culture.

An example from my own business illustrates this point. At my company, safety means everything, but we had an increase in driver accidents during the first half of 2010. Any insurance carrier would look at our long-term safety record and find the company in acceptable standing. However, with our culture of excellence in mind, we saw this increase in accidents as an unacceptable trend—and as an opportunity. In our business, we handle more than

44,000 freight movements per year. If a ninety-nine percent success rate is acceptable, then 440 service failures would be acceptable, too. But if we were content to accept that number of service failures, we might as well close our doors. When we took the time to look at our statistics, it became clear that perfection was the only acceptable goal.

When we realized we were not on the track for perfection—or even excellence—we knew something had to change in our culture. Making the commitment was easy, but knowing how to start was difficult. On a managerial level, our culture had evolved naturally up until that point. We worked hard to create a good work environment and provide excellent services, but there was not an active effort to define and communicate our culture to our employees. In management's view, if we were satisfied with being "good," we knew that we would be destined for extinction.

Rather than issue a memo, we issued a rallying cry designed to win our employees' hearts and minds. We began by raising awareness of the behaviors that were causing the negative trend in our success rates. We posted accident pictures on bulletin boards, asking for employee reactions that focused on what they would have done to prevent the accident. We cast a wide net beyond those with formal safety experience. Those in customer service submitted ideas about how more precise order-taking and directions could have prevented accidents or service failures. Mechanics identified maintenance and repair solutions. Everyone bought into the culture of stamping out mediocrity. We all committed to zero accidents on our watch, actively offering and executing solutions to prevent them.

In the end, we knew that we had to win our employees' hearts and minds so that they could elevate our performance. Culture was not something we could simply dictate. We had to be inclusive and consistent. We knew that we could not tolerate behavior that was out of line with our values, and so did our employees.

> To win over our employees, we had to make the case that perfection was the only acceptable measure for our service and safety standards. We offered them the following examples:
>
> If 99% was good enough . . .
>
> - Chicago O'Hare Airport would have two airplane accidents per day.
> - Twelve babies would be given to the wrong parents each day.
> - One hundred incorrect surgeries would be performed every day.
> - Jetco would have 440 service failures or accidents per year.

PART IV:

ANCHORING YOUR CULTURE

16

Keep the Journey Simple and Understandable

SIX MONTHS INTO OUR MISSION to develop a world-class company culture, our leadership team felt like we were rock stars. Everything was going our way, largely due to our efforts to proactively build our culture. Then, we began to see our progress slow down and, in some cases, regress.

We learned that the kick-off process is fun and relatively easy. After all, during the initial phase, the efforts are new and exciting for almost everyone. As with any new initiative, we had invested tremendous amounts of time and energy into the initial phase.

What we realized is that, once the honeymoon is over, the real work begins. Without a clear plan to anchor the culture, your path will begin to drift. Most likely, your company culture will drift back to its starting point, or worse. If the positive results disappear, employees can become cynical when they look at all of the effort they have put in to build a culture which failed.

Other challenges can threaten your journey to excellence, including company growth, employee turnover and, business cycles that cause unplanned change in your organization.

If you can successfully anchor your culture, then you will have an organization that transcends any single person or group, and can withstand the inevitable shocks it will encounter along the way. Once you have that vibrant culture, you will be able to invest your efforts into leading a shining company, as opposed to fighting daily fires.

It never ceases to amaze me how we complicate the simplest of ideas for ourselves. At its core, your culture is simply a function of your people and process working consistently and in harmony. Yet, when we gather people around the table, this simple issue becomes convoluted.

As you begin to anchor your culture, it is essential that you do not allow complex, long-term ideas to derail your program. It is a bit like trying to lose weight—if you set a long-term goal of losing thirty pounds, it may seem unattainable, and you may be tempted to stop trying with each setback. In contrast, if you keep the goal focused on the short term (one pound per week), success will be easier to recognize, and you will meet your long-term goal with fewer setbacks.

Many of us have seen this matrix for ranking ideas:

Easy to implement High Value	Difficult to implement High Value
Easy to implement Low Value	Difficult to implement Low Value

If you accept no other piece of advice from me as you embark upon your journey to build an excellent culture, keep your focus on the upper left quadrant of the matrix. Look for those actions you can take now that will have an immediate impact on your company and culture through a fast victory. Once you have momentum, then you can focus your efforts on longer-term, more complex, goals.

In my company, we experienced some early success implementing easy, high-value ideas. These ideas cost little and had a tremendous benefit. Here are a few examples:

Issue	Difficult High Value	Easy High Value
Management and front line are not in sync with each other.	Develop formal, written strategic plan. Roll out to team in company-wide meeting.	Conduct series of unscripted brown bag lunches allowing time for open discussion.
Quality is slipping.	Bring in outside consultants to assess operations and create study for continuous improvement.	Working side-by-side with employees, the internal team reviews the problem, determines root causes and forms action plan to solve.
Customer sales and satisfaction are on the decline.	Pay a lot of money for a formal survey. Make sure it is "blind" so that you don't know where the feedback comes from.	Get out of the office and into the field with real customers. Ask a very limited set of questions that allow for direct conversation.
Safety needs to improve.	Create a mountain to climb. If the company achieves safety excellence for one year, announce a generous reward.	Celebrate the steps along the way. After 30 days, bring in lunch. After 180 days, offer a small reward.

We have all been trained to aim for the "BHAG" (Big Hairy Audacious Goal). It is so drilled into our heads that we lose track of every step along the way. In most real-world situations, we achieve excellence in baby steps. It is important to understand that the process is not linear, and that setbacks are inevitable.

If you keep your focus on the easy, high-value steps, you will start to see results almost immediately. Initially, our culture initiative was created out of a desire to improve our safety performance. With this in mind, some of our easy, high-value steps included:

- Frequent small group meetings, known as "tailgate" sessions to promote frequent communication.
- Development of employee-owned brand, "Driving to Perfection" (D2P), which is a constant reminder of who we are and what we stand for.
- Monthly mailings to our employees' homes. These mailings cover an array of topics which are relevant to our employees and their family members. (For an example of mailings we sent home with our employees, see Chapters 21 and 26.)

17

Create an Internal Brand around Culture

AS ENTREPRENEURS, WE SPEND A fortune working on our brand. We wonder whether our value proposition is understood by our customers, or if it is too narrow or broad. Does our logo represent who we are? How about our ads—are they getting the message across? We hire marketing firms and consultants to demonstrate how we are different from our competition and why it matters—but most of our marketing effort is *outwardly* focused.

As important as it is to have a well-known external brand to draw in customers, it's equally (or more) important to ensure your brand values exist *inside* your organization. Your internal brand is your rallying cry. Every employee must know what the brand represents and be able to break it down through a concise summary of your company's culture and values.

As I mentioned earlier, at my company, our internal brand is "Driving to Perfection" (D2P). We have a logo and video testimonials to support the brand, and it appears on all employee correspondence and promotional items. We have discussed it enough among our employees that, if visitors ask anyone in our company what D2P means, they will get consistent answers.

Some of the video testimony we have in support of D2P is especially heartwarming. It shows employees discussing how they were pressured by previous employers to cut corners. They go on to explain that, within our culture, they have the freedom to do things the right way. Employees even discuss how they have taken our company values into their personal lives. For example, one individual told us how he used D2P when teaching his kids to drive.

Our internal brand has become a convenient vehicle with which to concisely repeat value-based messages several times per day.

Once you have built your internal brand and it is well understood, you can have some fun. Creative awards, T-shirts and recognition programs all are effective ways to build momentum for your new culture. The list of possibilities is endless for how you can promote your internal brand of culture and values to your team. However, remember: when developing an internal brand, it might be led by executives, but the brand itself is clearly driven by employees on a daily basis.

To create buy-in throughout our organization, we created a contest. We laid out the challenge: to develop a visual rallying cry that summarizes our culture and values. We received dozens of great ideas. From there, different teams narrowed the list down to five ideas that were presented to the entire company and then voted upon. Management led the process, but the employees owned and developed it.

Now, D2P is all over our company. It is the first thing our drivers see when entering their truck cabs and the last thing they see when exiting. D2P is a constant reminder of who we are as a company and what values we represent. However, while the constant visual reminders are important, success only comes by pairing words and images with consistent action throughout the organization. Our success using D2P as a rallying point for our entire organization is undeniable. But there certainly are many other effective internal branding campaigns.

While I was working for Waste Management, the company developed "Mission to Zero" (M2Z) as a rallying point to counter the company's declining safety performance. Its safety leaders didn't waste their time exclusively on creating handbooks and manuals that no one would read. Instead, the company focused on culture and the need to drive values all the way to the front lines. M2Z was the product of a series of related programs intended to promote value-based, safe behavior. The cornerstone of the M2Z program was called "Life Changer"—and included a video that told the story of a reckless truck driver and an even worse management team. The culmination of horrible decisions led to a needless and tragic fatality. Instead of sweeping the accident under the rug or paying the aggrieved widow a settlement to buy her silence, Waste Management actually partnered with the widow. She spoke about the tragedy to the entire Waste Management team. There was not a dry eye in the room. It was humbling to watch a typically macho group of people accept responsibility for the tragedy and vow to never let it happen again.

Using Life Changer to influence the company culture was a resounding success for Waste Management because it recognized this important truth: beliefs and emotions trump logic. We could have sat around the room and studied statistics or created policies and handbooks, with little or no impact. Instead, Life Changer was based on raw emotion—the recognition that our organization had needlessly caused a tragedy.

Had Life Changer only been mentioned in a one-time meeting, it would have had an impact, but the impact would have been temporary. The creation of the internal brand anchored the emotional impact of the need for safety into the company's DNA. M2Z and Life Changer became powerful internal brands. Every employee knew what they stood for:

- Taking ownership of your job
- Making value-based decisions
- Calling a critical and life-saving time out

A vibrant culture empowers employees to use their judgment in order to arrive at the right result. This is rarely accomplished through policy manuals or handbooks. Instead, it is accomplished through the "tribal" wisdom of the organization, where cultural behavior is transferred from one employee to the next through shared stories and behavior. Created with the input of every level of your company, your brand will become a reinforcement of your values and how your employees must conduct themselves in your organization.

18

Operationalize Your Values

AS YOU BEGIN TO ANCHOR your culture, remember that the best ideas in the world are meaningless without an implementation plan. Do you wonder why mission plans and vision statements have become a joke to employees? Often it is because they are hollow words. Leadership often spends time putting words on paper, but they spend little time breathing life into those words.

As an example, "accountability" is a core value at my company, and I trust it is a value at your business, as well. Without accountability, we condemn ourselves to make the same mistake repeatedly. Even worse, we develop a parent/child relationship with our employees, which is how we traditionally view accountability: Managers/parents hold the employees/children accountable.

We must create an environment where individuals and teams hold *each other* accountable. Yet accountability is the hardest value to consistently implement and uphold. Most of us view holding people accountable as an unpleasant task and are not very good at it.

Yet, all of this talk about accountability is meaningless without a plan to operationalize the value. During our journey to a better culture, we have used the following ideas to operationalize accountability:

Documenting Service Issues

Every time we have a service issue, it must be documented. An email is then automatically sent to our entire team in this format.

```
----Original Message-----
From: Jetco Operating System
Sent: Friday, March 01, 2013 12:07 PM
To: Everyone
Subject: Service Issue
Service Issue Notification
Created by: L Jones
PRO     : 471748.1
Date    : 03/01/13
Time    : 12:04
Customer : Pipe and Tube Supply
PRO Owner: Billy Johnson
Issues  : Customer Service/Booking Error
Desc    : customer dispatched 6 pc shipment to Jetco. Only 4 of the 6 pcs
were collected.

Resolved : Collecting material from Consolidated Warehouse.
Transportation costs will not be charged to customer.
```

At first, some of my managers objected to this Draconian process. How could we possibly broadcast one person's error to the team? A funny thing happened. As we disseminated these issues, our team engaged in healthy discussion. Team members began to check each other's work. They looked for the root cause(s) of the errors. The team rose to the challenge.

No one likes to see his or her name associated with a service issue, and they came to each other's support.

Bonuses and Reviews

An occasional review is no substitution for the daily feedback and interaction that is essential to a healthy culture. However, formal reviews provide an opportunity to operationalize accountability. We have enhanced the effectiveness of our review process with the following changes:

> *Reviews are held quarterly.* If you wait for an annual review to address service issues, it is usually a waste of time. Most employees—and we, as managers—need feedback much more regularly. Quarterly feedback allows employees to build on their successes and make required course corrections, often before it is too late.

> *Reviews focus on three areas of performance: company, team, and individual.* Each employee must be cognizant of not only his or her performance, but also that of his or her team and the company. If the review focuses only on the individual, you may wind up with a superstar on a sinking ship.

> *Each quarterly review is accompanied by a bonus opportunity.* If you pay bonuses annually, Christmas is an eternity away on January 1. In my company, bonuses are tied to company, individual, and team performance. Managers receive a gross amount that they may allocate among their teams. I learn a lot about

a manager by how he or she allocates his or her bonus pool. Many managers do not like the unpleasant task of telling low-performing employees that they will not receive a bonus. So, they will find money for these people by reducing the amounts awarded to better performers, promoting a culture of mediocrity and undermines accountability. My better managers do not fear giving difficult messages while differentiating among their employees.

Managers gain my respect by making the tough decisions—rewarding the stars and challenging others to improve. Some managers fear that differentiation will cause people on the lower end of the spectrum to leave. But, after a few quarters at the bottom, isn't that what we want anyway?

When I think about operationalizing accountability, I have to admit that it is a weakness of mine. Sometimes, I prefer to fix the immediate problem, instead of dealing with the more complicated and beneficial challenge of weaving the value into the culture. For me, the failure to operationalize accountability looks like this:

- "It is easier to fix the problem myself than to teach you how to fix it."
- Allowing the employee to come to me with an issue with another employee before forcing them to work it out between themselves. (This is the parent-child syndrome.)
- Sugar-coating—not calling out the bad behaviors that undermine accountability.

When you look closer, it becomes obvious that the missing piece to most value statements is the accompanying plan to operationalize these values—to bring them to life. In the above example, our company could talk about accountability all day long. The talk would be meaningless without daily behaviors that support and add meaning to the values. If you are spending your time developing a value statement without an operating plan, you may end up doing more harm than good. You could find yourself communicating a set of values to your employees that nobody is required to live. This exercise makes the value statement a subject of ridicule, instead of one of inspiration.

What you define as your values—and how you choose to operationalize them—is up to you. No matter what, you must understand the importance of breathing life into those values.

The following is my company's value statement:

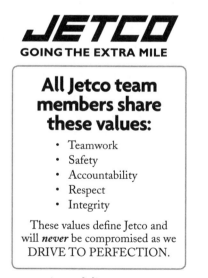

JETCO
GOING THE EXTRA MILE

All Jetco team members share these values:

- Teamwork
- Safety
- Accountability
- Respect
- Integrity

These values define Jetco and will *never* be compromised as we DRIVE TO PERFECTION.

jetcodelivery.com

This value statement would be meaningless without a plan to operationalize it. After all, is there any business that would not list integrity as a value? But do you believe that every company conducts its business with integrity? A value statement is at the core of a vibrant culture *only if* your team is actually held accountable for living and breathing the values. Here are some additional examples of how we operationalized some of our values.

Value	Concrete Actions to Operationalize Values
Teamwork	• Written processes and procedures so that each team member knows the team's mission and his or her role on the team. • Bonus plan that contains a balance between individual and team performance. Encourage individual excellence but not at the expense of the team. • Productive team meetings with broad participation focused on continuous improvement. • Call out behaviors that undermine the team. Look especially for politics and finger-pointing, and stop these unproductive behaviors immediately.
Integrity	• Do not allow even the tiniest of lies to go unnoticed. If you have a customer service problem, admit fault quickly, apologize, and fix the problem. Tolerating one lie paves the way for thousands more. • Don't make a deal if you cannot honor it. So many agreements are made to get the deal done, even if you doubt your ability to perform. This is especially true with some employers who lure employees in with pie in the sky promises. • Ensure that there is no appearance that your company lacks integrity. We all know that the rumor mill works 24/7. If you or your organization is falsely confronted with an appearance of dishonesty, confront it immediately.
Respect	• Create an environment that encourages fierce and open debate. Set the ground rules up front; that way, debate cannot become a personal attack. • The greatest respect that you can show is to acknowledge that an individual is a human being first and an employee second. Promoting a proper work-life balance for all employees shows a simple respect for people's lives outside the business.

**Don't let your mission and value
statements become a bad joke!**

Your mission statement is your stake in the ground. It lets your employees know why you exist. Your values are the glue that binds you together.

Many companies pour tremendous resources into the development and rollout of their mission and value statements. Don't simply post them on the wall—treat them like living, breathing members of your workforce.

Devote time to *operationalizing* your mission and values.

19

The Integration Process

AS YOU ANCHOR YOUR CULTURE, understand that every time a new employee joins your workforce, the culture changes. Each new hire brings a wealth of experience and habits that will impact your culture—for better or worse.

Knowing whether someone is a fit within your culture is vital. Think about most of our orientation programs. They probably sound something like "Meet your supervisor . . . The bathroom is over there . . . Read this 200-page manual."

You must change your mindset about orientation in two ways. First, orientation should be about your company's unique culture. Second, orientation should *not* be a one-day (or one-week) program. Rather, it should be an on-going process.

When we bring someone new on at Jetco, we spend a significant amount of our orientation time on our values and why we perform our functions a certain way.

To anchor our culture for each new hire, we do the following:

- We have produced a video entitled "What Does D2P Mean to Me?"—a candid collection of employee testimonials regarding our company's culture. Through this, the new hire is exposed to the "Jetco Way" immediately.

- Every new hire meets with a senior executive. While it may seem like common sense, leaders must take the time to meet new hires. More often than not, our new employees have said, "In all of my past jobs, I have never spoken to the president of my company. Here, he met me on day one."

- When I meet with new employees, I try to get to know them personally. I lock onto the soccer coach, the part-time minister, the family person. From a business standpoint, I want to know why the employee left his or her previous employer and what attracted him or her to our company. Not surprisingly, in most cases I find that cultural issues drove the employee out. "They didn't treat me right," or "I was at the bottom of the rung," or "No respect," are common complaints. When we are not at our best, these are the reasons people leave us, as well.

- Every new hire is assigned a mentor. Our mentors know the "Jetco Way," and they are the cultural lifeline to the new employee. There is no such thing as asking your mentor a dumb question. We have been known to experience a disproportionate amount of turnover during the first twelve months of employment. The mentor program is designed to chase out the ghosts and allow for a solid foundation to be built between the company and new employees.

- We host a "new-hire breakfast" monthly. This breakfast is a roundtable discussion with a few of our senior leaders. A few months into the employee's tenure with the company, we want to know how we are doing. (Is our orientation program working? Have we kept our promises?) These breakfasts allow for a continual process of improvement, engagement, and healthy course correction—both for the employees and for the company.

By properly integrating the employee into the culture—as opposed to performing simple job training—you are increasing the odds of an excellent new hire. Moreover, you are also weeding out—at the earliest possible stage—those who may harm your culture.

20

A Simple, Written Affirmation

AS YOUR COMPANY'S CULTURE, VALUES, and code of conduct solidify, it is important to have written documentation. I am not talking about a heavy-duty handbook. Instead, I recommend a simple, one-page commitment. This is a "culture contract" between your employees and the company.

Take my "Driving to Perfection" commitment as an example:

DRIVING TO PERFECTION
My Commitment

Driving to Perfection embodies who we are as a company. D2P is a constant reminder of Jetco's core values and beliefs. D2P guides our every action.

As a member of the Jetco team, **I commit**:

- To live and embrace our core <u>values</u>: Safety, Honesty, Integrity, Respect, Teamwork, Communication and Accountability.

- To put safe operations above all else. "Zero" is the <u>only</u> acceptable result when measuring accidents and injuries. Through my actions, Jetco will achieve "Zero."

- To follow the car in front of me as if my family and loved ones are in it. I will always keep my distance and adjust my speed and space under the circumstances.

- To fully appreciate the risk of my job. I will plan and anticipate. I will always wear my PPE and be fully aware of my surroundings.

- To eliminate all distractions when driving or performing any other safety–sensitive function.

- To take my time and "do it right." When in doubt, I will call a time out!

- To take care of myself and my equipment.

By signing this commitment, I understand my role at Jetco. I accept my responsibility to create a safe environment for the entire Jetco team. With my commitment we are Driving to Perfection!

_____   _____
Jetco Team Member   Manager

This written affirmation is essential because we are all human. We will have bad days when our behaviors deviate from company values. When coaching an employee who deviated from our core values, I encourage my managers to pull the culture contract out of the file. When we meet with the wayward employee, we remind him or her of our values and of how we do things at our company. We also remind the employee that we all agreed in writing on a code of conduct. Normally, this reminder is all the employee needs, and it is much more effective than overused disciplinary tactics such as write-ups and suspension.

As you can see from my example, our contract is focused on safety-sensitive functions. (After all, when driving 80,000-pound loads around the city, safety is paramount.) Your company's cultural contract should capture the non-negotiable values and behaviors required for an employee to thrive in your company. Anything more than one page will dilute your message and become overkill.

Always remember that your culture contract is your bond with your employees. It eliminates the chance for anyone (from the front-line to the executive office) to use the excuse that he or she was not informed about those items that are most precious to your business.

Sometimes you need a written affirmation between you and yourself. This is my own daily reminder. It is a positive affirmation of how I look when performing at my peak. What would yours look like?

Reminder to Brian—my role at Jetco is to:

- Listen—above all else!
- Lead
- Motivate
- Support

- Train
- Develop
- Plan
- Grow
- Innovate
- Educate
- Learn
- Inspire
- Question
- Communicate
- My actions need to be consistent with our vision, values, and purpose.
- If I can devote my time to filling this role, then everyone on the Jetco team will realize our full potential.
- I have a championship team, and we have mutual respect.
- I love my people and I am interested in all of them
- There is a lot of trust in Jetco.

21

Drive Your Culture Home— Literally

AS WE HAVE ANCHORED OUR culture at Jetco, we have learned that getting through to our employees is simply the beginning of the mission. If you focus on your employees and ignore their families, full cultural alignment is nearly impossible.

Here's why: In today's world, our family and friends are never more than a text, tweet, or Facebook message away. Even so, you want your employee's head to be fully in the game as he or she performs his or her mission's critical duties for your organization. This may be challenging if a demanding family member is continually in contact.

What are your choices? Restrict Internet access? With smartphones, the employee probably does not need your Internet anyway. Check in all mobile devices at the beginning of the work day? Not happening.

The only way to ensure that your employees are able to put their full time and focus into the company is to ensure that their families are fully in line with your culture. How do you bring the families into the culture? Let's skip the hated annual company picnic. At their best, picnics might involve a hot dog, a carnival ride, and a fast exit. At their worst, everyone must attend, but nobody *wants* to attend.

Instead, try these ideas:

- Make regular contact instead of the annual show. In our case, we send a monthly mailing to our employee's homes. The mailing focuses on topics that are of general interest, but that also have a clear tie into the company's values and mission. Here is one of my favorites:

DRIVE YOUR CULTURE HOME—LITERALLY

GOING THE EXTRA MILE

Dear Jetco Team:

As many of you know, I am Jetco's outside salesperson. A lot of my time is spent driving. On Friday, August 13, 2010, I was almost killed by another company's truck.

The truck and I were driving northbound on Highway 59 at Little York. The truck was loaded with a heavy piece on the left lane, and I was stuck in the center lane. For no apparent reason, the truck swerved into my lane. Fortunately, the right lane was open, and I was able to steer clear of the truck.

As I watched the truck drive, it continued to jump the lanes. I caught up with the truck and honked to get the driver's attention. I don't think the driver heard my horn. When I pulled up to the truck, here is what I saw:

THE DRIVER WAS BUSY TEXTING ON HIS PHONE!

For a long time, Jetco has warned us about the dangers of cell phone use, texting and emailing — as well as distracted driving in general. Now I have firsthand experience as to why this is so important. When you are driving for Jetco, please put all of your attention on the road. As trucking industry professionals, we are the "White Knights" of the road. Family members — please help your loved ones by **NOT texting or calling them while driving. Professional drivers must devote 100% of their attention to their jobs. If not, the results could be tragic.**

I was almost killed. Please learn from my experience.

Sincerely,

Hubert Flores

Hubert Flores

This letter has a clear emotional appeal because a well-loved employee was almost killed by someone who was texting while driving. In addition, the letter underscores an important business point—distractions, no matter your job, can have disasterous consequences.

- If you do want to have a company event, instead of having an off-site event, stage it at your location. How many times do our families really get to see how their loved ones spend a majority of their waking hours? Allow for "show and tell." This will tie everyone into a positive experience at your facility and help the family members understand the organization's direction. If you propose this idea and encounter significant resistance, it might be a strong suggestion that you need to look into the level of employee pride.

- Be liberal when sharing information about the financial strength of your company. Make people understand that they are on a winning team.

- Sell your company to the families as aggressively as you sell to your customers. Let's say that an employee receives an offer to work for a competitor at a five percent increase. Are your employees and their families armed with enough data to make an accurate comparison?

- Be sure you are providing an outstanding company work environment. Can a supportive family member help the employee compare what you offer to the "devil that you do not know?" Be sure that the whole family knows what you offer in terms of intangibles, like a happy, desirable place to work.

From an emotional, financial and business perspective, anchoring your culture must involve frequent, repetitive, and focused contact not just with the people you see every day, but also with employees' family members. Executed correctly, you will have a whole army working to build and support your company culture.

I encourage you to examine the level of connection that your company has with employees' families. If the connection is not frequent or strong, perhaps the ideas in this chapter will allow you to create a beneficial bond.

22

Focused, Developed Technology Promotes Your Culture

WHEN IT COMES TO TECHNOLOGY, I will admit it: I am hooked. I am fascinated by how much technology has improved our lives. Yes, I like to be at the front of the line when the new toys are released. But, that is in my personal life. My view towards technology is very different in my business life. Each day, there is a dizzying array of technological advances that can consume your team's time and resources, only to be obsolete tomorrow. Most of us know stories about companies pouring millions of dollars into a technology initiative, only to scrap it later.

I invest in technology when it is sufficiently mature and after it has been proven that it can serve as a means to help us accomplish our mission. Technology, for us, is a means to an end. You don't need a "solution" if a problem does not exist. In our company, we view software as a service, not a product. Taken a step further, software is simply our standard operating procedures translated into code. This sounds fairly basic; however, an astounding number of businesspeople view software as a "plug-and-play" product. And, for simple or routine tasks, plug-and-play may be enough.

However, to operate a process-driven business and to differentiate your business from the competition in the eyes of your customers, you must view software as part of your secret ingredient. Technology can be a key component to your company's culture, and the ability to customize *practical* technology is essential for your internal operation, as well as for your customers.

Let me provide you with a few real-life examples of what caused us to invest in upgraded hardware and software.

The Challenge	The Investment	The Result
Losing track of trucks in the field. Too much time screaming into those old Nextel radios.	GPS installed in trucks.	We know where our trucks are located down to the street corner. We can then provide more reliable information to our customers.
Spending tremendous amounts of time responding to routine customer requests for load status and documents.	Created "Virtual Dispatch" Oracle-based platform, allowing transparency into our system.	Customers can access what they need, when they need it, including documents and real-time status updates. Saves tremendous amounts of time for customers and us.
We operate in a safety-sensitive business, where one dispatch mistake can result in a serious outcome.	Custom programmed a series of "hooks" in the system, which match properly qualified drivers to loads.	Reduced potential for costly error. Our software is our tool for ensuring compliance with our processes and procedures.

These are just a few examples of how technology has improved our business, but I hope that you see my point. If you invest properly in new technology with the end results in mind, you can promote efficiency throughout your company and strengthen your bonds with your customers.

If you are not yet at a point where customized programming makes sense, keep the same principles in mind when buying packaged software. You will find products that can handle your accounting and basic functionality. Look for the package that is most closely aligned with your needs. Your business is unique, and you should ensure that your equipment furthers your mission and that you do not become a slave to your system!

One final tip: when developing or purchasing customer-facing systems, be sure to invite your key customers for beta-testing. You may be able to determine what your customer needs without assembling a focus group, but bringing him or her in makes your customer a partner in the process.

In many cases, Jetco's focused development of technology is what sets us apart. Technology is an investment, not an expense. Software is a service, not a product. Done right, upgraded technology is a phenomenal tool to de-commoditize your business. I have trucks. So does my competitor. I have good drivers. So does my competitor. I can let you see the truck with your shipment on Google Maps, providing complete transparency during and after the completion of your critical shipment. Suddenly, the competition doesn't seem as fierce.

23

Your Culture and the Community

MANY OF US HAVE BEEN through the annual shake-down where we are asked to support a charity adopted by our company's CEO or other executive. Dutifully, we write our checks, but it's less about doing good and more about not making waves so that we can stay in the good graces of the powers that be.

While our donations are almost certainly put to good use, the act of giving becomes an empty corporate ritual that is often resented. Even so, I strongly believe that every company has a role in the greater community, and it is our duty to give back.

I have often been disappointed by how impersonal the process of charitable giving has become. I challenge you to follow a different path to achieve greater meaning by giving back to those aspects of the community which are important to your employees and, at the same time, elevating your culture.

For corporate participation in community activities to be truly meaningful to the entire company, employees must be engaged and enthusiastic. Once there is employee engagement, community participation creates a unique bond among the employees, the company, and the community.

Here is what Jetco does to engender *meaningful* community participation:

First, the bulk of our community activities are employee driven. This includes a wide spectrum of work with charities, youth sports, church activities, fun runs, and other events. Sure, we could concentrate our spending on one charity in a way that would allow me to be the hero and raise my own profile, but that is not what this is about. A community program that drives employee pride, corporate culture, and connection to the company should be as diverse as the employee base itself. Our employees lead us to community-driven events, and we do not force anyone to participate in programs that have no meaning for them.

Secondly, we look for programs that involve more than just a monetary donation. When certain charities need a truck, Jetco is there. Our employees have been involved with backpack collections, food drives, and Boys & Girls Club Christmas parties, just to name a few. In one case, we used two semis to deliver bicycles to kids in need; one of our drivers was moved to tears during his participation. He told me that the event triggered memories of his childhood and it made him proud to work at a company that is dedicated to making a difference in the lives of others. Of course, his reaction and pride in what we were doing spread like wildfire throughout the company.

When thinking about community service, think of it is a low-cost investment with a tremendous payback. Because your time is often as important as your money, community service does not need to be a budget-busting proposition. Done right, the connection that you promote within your company, as well as between your employees and the community, is guaranteed to drive pride *and* loyalty.

PART V:

CULTURE AND YOUR EMPLOYEES

24

Cultural Compensation: What Matters is What They Can't Buy

ONE OF MY MENTORS TAUGHT me that "people covet most that which they cannot buy." In my experience, this translates into people seeking appreciation and recognition that they matter as a human being above anything else. Sincere, genuine, and consistent care for employees will result in loyalty and limitless dedication to achievement.

I'm not suggesting a free-for-all without concern for profitability, safety, quality, or service. I'm suggesting a well-defined culture focused on success and security for all. If we all believe in and share a set of values as a means of doing business, then we will protect and nurture those values, knowing they will lead to individual and company success. This goes beyond just showing appreciation. Doing the right things in the right way—and recognizing those behaviors—advances the company's culture and creates an environment in which people want to work, succeed, and dedicate themselves to perpetuating that culture.

So why do many of us face constant morale issues that lead to negative perceptions and valuable-but-disengaged employees who are thinking of leaving us? Instead of focusing on the easy and superficial—such as a new office, title, or laptop—focus on creating an outstanding work environment, with a special and unique culture that employees embrace and own. This is where the long-term benefits reside, as the following example illustrates.

Building Rapport

A nearby business owner and I had made plans to meet over lunch. An hour before, he called with two options. Either we could reschedule, or we could meet at his office, where his employees had organized a lunch to celebrate the Houston Texans' first playoff game. As simple as this may sound, clearly it was important to him—and his employees—for him to be there. We decided to meet at his office, where the lunchroom was filled with employees mingling over hot dogs and potato chips. Shortly after we entered the room, I could tell that the employees appeared genuinely comfortable around their boss. My friend introduced me to each of his employees. Not only did he know everyone by name—from employees from the warehouse to the office and drivers—he knew something about each person.

I could tell that this level of mutual respect and rapport came about through leading by example and human interaction. My friend had tapped into the special need that each of us has to be recognized and appreciated. He did not spend a ton of time and money to hire outside consultants to tell him to be genuine. In fact, it only cost him the time it took to share hot dogs and potato chips at that party.

Admittedly, this is the nice-to-have, fuzzy stuff that some people dismiss when they think of culture initiatives. These people do not understand. Most of my friend's employees have long tenures at the company and turnover has never been an issue. Because his company puts employees first and does not have to fight the "revolving door," they put their energy into simply running and growing the business.

Ironically, the least expensive actions we take often have the greatest rewards. To ensure that your employees feel relevant and appreciated, try a few of these ideas:

- Ensure that you "shout out" acts of excellence. Don't wait for seismic events. Look for everyday demonstrations of people living your values. Look for translations of those values into measureable results.
- Assemble informally in small groups for lunch. The agenda needs to be unstructured. Listen to the team talk about their successes, challenges, and aspirations. Get to know your team on a personal level. If

needed, break the ice with simple questions. An example might be: *What is the most significant event that you experienced in the last ninety days?*

- Always follow up with the team. Your employees will stop coming to you with ideas if there is no follow up. When employees have ideas to increase profit or to boost morale or to save cost, they are telling you that they care deeply about your company. Make sure that you show them that you feel the same way.

25

Money Matters

HOW MANY TIMES HAVE GOOD employees left your company over pay? Clearly, there are times when money *does* matter. The employee may be stepping into a new career or position, perhaps one that you cannot offer or match. In those cases, we can only wish the employees well and thank them for their service.

The larger problem occurs when employees accept *similar*, lateral-move positions with your competitors. The employee may tell you that he or she is being offered more money, and that may be true. However, I am willing to bet that you pay your employees within the same market range as your competitors. Assuming this is true, why would an employee leave the security of your company in exchange for an unknown position with a competitor? It is not about the money. No matter what your employee's supervisors tell you and no matter what the departing employee tells you, satisfied employees rarely make lateral moves due to compensation.

When you start to hear valued employees complain about the compensation, you need to listen carefully. Something is out of line in your culture. The issue may be confined to a particular department or manager, or the issue may have spread to your whole organization. If you dig deep enough, you will find that some basic human need of your departing employee has not been met.

In the trucking industry, average annual turnover is 80–100 percent. That means our industry is rotating its entire staff of drivers annually. My company has been fortunate to have a turnover rate that is a fraction of the industry average. Nevertheless, we recently experienced an unprecedented level of employee departures.

Determined to get to the bottom of the problem, we examined whether we had lost sight of the market. Were we, in fact, underpaying our team? To analyze the problem, we conducted exit interviews, knowing that some employees would not participate, while others would sugarcoat their reasons for leaving. During the exit interviews, we laid out our company values and asked one question: *While you were an employee, were you treated in line with these values?*

We learned that we were unintentionally failing to uphold two of our most important values: trust and integrity. Our drivers are paid a percentage of the invoice paid by the customer, and we knew that our payments were accurate. But, due to the way that our driver settlement reports were set up, it appeared we were not playing fairly with them. After reviewing the situation, we found that either clear communication had not been a priority to us, or we had been blind to the issue. Either way, we had created the perception that we lacked integrity. Because of this, we lost some valuable team members. Without question, our drivers were right in how they perceived us.

Fortunately, accountability is also a core value of our company. We owned up to the problem and revamped our settlement process. Along the way, we involved a cross-functional team to ensure complete transparency in our interactions. As a result of this experience, we are now stronger and have a better bond with our employees, but this lesson definitely came at a high cost.

Earlier, I proposed that employees rarely accept a lateral job simply for more money. Employees may use money as their stated reason for departure, but, if you dig deeper, you are bound to find different actual reasons for their departures. Unfortunately, if you are relying on the exit interview to find out what is going on, it is probably too late to change the situation.

We conducted a survey of our employees to ask what they appreciate most about our company. Non-monetary factors took first place. In particular, employees pointed to the enjoyment and recognition they received from team celebrations and praise from senior leadership.

We came to the conclusion that employees were most likely to leave when we violated one of the "Three Ts":

- Treatment
- Transparency
- Trust

Treatment

It only makes sense that an employee will leave if he or she is treated poorly. When we think of poor treatment, we think of the obvious examples: rudeness, profanity, etc. The real examples of poor treatment are much more subtle and destructive.

In our company, we saw poor treatment manifest itself through a failure of management to follow up on employee concerns or ideas. When a manager doesn't follow up, he or she is telling that employee that the employee is not important. If the manager has not made the effort to understand the employee's priorities, the employee is not likely to stay.

This type of poor treatment leads the employee to believe that he or she is anonymous and does not matter. As a result, good employees leave *managers*, not companies—but the overall impact is the same.

Transparency

All employees have a need to belong—to feel they are part of their company. If an employee believes that everything happens behind closed doors, team members will become disconnected. As I indicated earlier, our employees are paid on their productivity. Yet, their settlement reports provided no detail regarding how we actually calculated their pay. We realized that we were not being transparent regarding an issue of vital concern to our employees.

As we embraced the problem, we threw open our books. The "black box" disappeared, and our employees now have full access to their payroll information. In a word, we became transparent. But this is not all.

Transparency extends throughout our company— from sales figures to customer shout-outs to service problems. Our employees know what is going on at *their* company at all times. Without a doubt, this has created a new and more positive environment within our company.

Trust

If treatment or transparency is lacking in your company, trust will surely suffer. Without trust, your company will be unable to build a vibrant culture. Employees will work against each other, instead of as a team. Trust is your most precious asset and is at the foundation of your ability to manage your company's performance.

Since we started looking in the mirror and addressing the Three Ts, we have strengthened the ties between our employees and managers and have created a greater sense of belonging in the company.

Not surprisingly, this has also translated to greater *customer* satisfaction. In the past year, we have tripled—and, in some cases, quadrupled—the amounts that certain key customers spend with us. The amount of time you invest in strengthening what happens on the inside will undoubtedly pay dividends on the outside.

Ideas for building on the Three Ts

Once you accept the idea that the Three Ts are at the core of employee satisfaction, production, and reputation, you will be able to develop the plan that works best for your company. Here are a few ideas to get you started:

- Ensure your managers make time to learn about their team members as human beings, not just as employees.
- Don't be afraid to open the books. Share key data points regularly. Allow your employees to share the joy of the victories, as well as to be a part of the solution to the problems.
- Throw out the suggestion box and replace it with regular listening sessions. The box is too frequently

used as a way of telling an employee to write down an idea because we are too busy to listen. Leaders in search of a positive culture must be available to listen—and then follow up. Even if an employee's idea is not practical, we all need to at least extend him or her the courtesy of knowing that the idea has been heard.

- Ensure that your words and actions always line up. By saying one thing and doing another, you will never be able to build trust. Trust comes from speaking and acting consistently.

- Repeat! Becoming transparent and building trust is a daily task. It will not work if you only give employees good treatment once in a while. You need to repeat this over and over again. Reinforcing the Three Ts should be one of our key functions as leaders.

26

Promoting the Big Picture

IN THE PREVIOUS CHAPTER, I argued that employees rarely make lateral career moves for the money and that we need to take a closer look to find out what is really going on if this is what we are being told is going on.

A flip-side exists. Imagine two rooms. In the first room, a group of employees is complaining about their pay. In the second room, a group of managers is complaining about the employees' complete lack of gratitude, asking "Don't these people understand everything we do for them?" The answer is easy: probably not.

It is not practical for employees to know the value of their overall pay package . . . unless you tell them. Benefits are important. It is not enough to say "We offer health insurance and a 401(k)." Be sure your employees and their families know the *value* of working at your company. Shout it out— bang the drum!

If employees are considering other employment options, they may compare their current salaries to those offered by the prospective new employers. But base salary is only one data point. All of the other benefits are often overlooked and not quantified by the wayward employees. This is where you must provide the employees with the tools to make a proper comparison.

The following is a letter that we mailed to all of our employees. We mailed it so that my employees *and their family members* could all understand the overall benefit package that we offer. If the decision to change jobs is discussed at the dinner table, then all of the reasons to stay should be discussed, too.

GOING THE EXTRA MILE

Dear Jetco Family,

As you know, Jetco is on a mission to be a world-class company — to provide our customers and employees with the best level of service we can offer. This mission starts and ends with us being a world-class employer. We cannot be a great company and provide a high level of service without your participation, and sometimes, we do not adequately share all of our efforts — both big and small — to create a world-class work environment for you.

THE JETCO ADVANTAGE

Exceptional Benefits

- **Humana Health Insurance.** We pay up to $411 per month of the cost of premium. More than 70% of eligible employees have elected to enroll in health insurance.
- **401(k).** If you contribute 5% of your salary, we match 80%. In other words, $100 becomes $180 on day one! Unlike many other 401(k) plans, you are fully vested in your contribution and our match. Nothing is ever subject to forfeiture.
- **Dental Insurance.** We pay 50% of the cost of our DHMO plan.
- **Life Insurance.** $20,000 free life insurance for health insurance enrollees.
- **Optional life, vision and disability insurance.**

Safety First – D2P Protects You!

Of course, we value safety above all else — both yours and that of the public. Our commitment extends beyond this promise.

- As a professional driver, you have a Personal Safety Profile (PSP) that is monitored by the federal government. A clean PSP is your ticket to the best careers in the industry. Jetco (along with many other quality employers) requires excellent PSPs. In fact, we reject 80% of our job applicants as a result of poor PSPs.
- Because we believe in D2P, we also believe in protecting your PSP. For more information on your PSP, visit http://www.psp.fmcsa.dot.gov.
- We recognize and reward excellence through quarterly and annual safety bonuses. We have paid bonuses, without fail, every quarter since beginning the program in 2007.

A Winning Team

- Jetco is here to support you for the long term. We've been in business since 1976, and have solid financial credentials, meaning we have the financial security to pay your salary on time and invest our profits back into the company.
- Another way in which we show our commitment to you is by providing you with job stability through poor economic times. During the Great Recession, Jetco did not lay off a single employee. Since then, we have enjoyed excellent growth with you in mind.

As always, I'm always open for discussion or any questions as we continue to grow and strengthen the Jetco Advantage. Thanks for being a vital part of the Jetco family.

Sincerely,

Brian Fielkow

JETCO BY THE NUMBERS

Years of Service	% of Employees
0 – 1	34%
1 – 5	38%
5 +	28%

We're grateful to team members who have devoted such a meaningful portion of their careers to the D2P team!

As you can see, this letter is very focused on our company—and what we bring to the table—but it also points out that we appreciate long-term employees.

What would your communication look like? How would you promote your business to your employees and their families? If you are not aggressively selling the comprehensive value of working at your company, then who will? Spending time developing your unique employee value proposition—and making sure it is uniformly understood—is a big part of creating a positive culture.

27

Testing for the Perfect Fit

I HAVE LEARNED TO HIRE for aptitude and culture rather than for base skills, and I use assessment profiles for any key hires. At one point in my career, I did not put a lot of stock in these assessments. I have, since, learned that I was wrong to dismiss them!

A few years ago, I hired an accountant. The interview was terrific and the call back was even better. He passed the skills test administered by our outside CPA. Our team loved him. It turned out to be one of the worst hiring decisions I have ever made.

We had administered a "Caliper" profile test, but basically ignored it. (When using a Caliper profile test, the resulting Caliper profile can provide valuable insight into any candidate's behavioral traits, but this is only helpful if you pay attention to it.) We mentally convinced ourselves that there was no way the Caliper could vary so dramatically from what our "eyes and ears" told us, and we decided to believe our instincts, instead of the facts.

Here are a few observations from that employee's Caliper test results:

- "When faced with unusual or complicated problems, he might have to seek assistance . . . His potential to handle complexity may warrant further exploration."
- The candidate "does not display leadership dynamics in terms of directing, delegating, or holding others accountable."
- "He may not be able to assess financial issues from a big-picture perspective. He probably would struggle to develop important processes."

I am here to tell you that these predictions were one hundred percent accurate. Had we taken the time to review this data before rushing to hire the person who had otherwise charmed us, we could have avoided untold, mutual, dissatisfaction. At least we learned.

We happily employed the Caliper test on the replacement search. The replacement candidate "display[ed] the abstract reasoning ability to grasp complex work problems and [was] unlikely to overlook information that could affect his judgment." The candidate also "[was] inclined to hold others accountable for their performance and could be viewed as demanding." In essence, the Caliper predicted a perfect match.

Once again, the test was one hundred percent accurate, and this hire was a resounding success. I am not suggesting that any profile assessment is a substitute for a rigorous, in-depth and culture-based interview process. Nothing will take the place of the interview. However, an outside assessment will uncover traits and inclinations you are almost certain to overlook.

Still unsure about the validity of testing? Take an assessment test yourself. See what it indicates about you. Show a close friend, co-worker, or family member and ask whether the description is accurate.

If I have convinced you to use assessment tests, I will most likely have helped you avoid a costly mistake down the road. But that is just the first step. You can also use assessments to improve the dynamics among the individuals on your team.

For example, my leadership team all took assessments and then met to review each other's results. Through doing so, we gained greater insight into how each of us is likely to behave. Our internal assessments were the springboard for greater understanding and teamwork.

Of course, no test could possibly replace your own judgment and instinct when hiring. That said, during interviews many of us ask questions about a candidate's skills or job history. We do not ask questions that provide a window into the candidate's likely behavioral responses to your environment or the specific demands of your culture.

I realize that some people are skilled at bluffing their way through interviews. My Vistage chair, John N. Younker, PhD, gave me the following list of topics to discuss and questions to ask during the interview process. Because they focus on numerous diverse areas, I have found that these questions elicit responses that provide a useful window into each candidate's likely behavior.

Self-Regard

Please describe what you consider to be your greatest strength, and provide an example of where you recently exhibited this strength.

Please describe what you consider to be your greatest weakness, and provide an example of where you recently exhibited this weakness.

Assertiveness
Tell me about the last time you disagreed with someone. What was the situation and what was the outcome?

Interpersonal Relationships
Tell me about the last time you entered an environment or group where you were new. What did you do to become known?

Stress Tolerance
Describe a time when you were under a great deal of stress. What caused the stress, and what actions did you take to resolve the situation?

Impulse Control
When was the last time you were very angry? What caused you to be angry, and how did you resolve the situation?

Problem Solving
Please describe the last time you were faced with a large problem. What did you do to deal with it?
Can you give me an example—step by step—of how you handled a difficult problem at work or at home?

Happiness
Tell me about the best thing that has happened to you in the past five years. Why do you value it so much?

Creativity/Innovation
Please describe the two best ideas you came up with at your current or most recent company. What generated these ideas? What were the end results of the ideas? Who did you have to convince regarding the value of these ideas? Where do they stand now?

Teamwork
Tell me about the last time you worked in a team. When and where was this? What was the purpose for the team and what was your role?

Whom within the team did you have the most difficulty communicating with and relating to and why? What actions did you take to cause the working relationship to improve?

Time Management/Commitment/Dedication
Tell me about a time when you needed to invest extra time and energy to get a job completed or project finished. What did you do to finish the job or project? How often did—or does—this occur?

Communication
Where and when have you communicated and worked the most with customers or service providers? What was the most difficult of these relationships and why? What steps did you take to improve the relationship?

Leadership/Delegation
Please describe the last time you were in a leadership role, either officially or unofficially. What was the greatest challenge you encountered in this role and relationship? What did you

do to facilitate your goal and the relationships involved?

Project Management

Please describe a time when you were responsible for a project from the initial stages through completion. What other staff members worked with you and what were their roles? What were the greatest challenges you encountered through the project? What did you do or develop to overcome these challenges? Whom did you report to on this project and what was the style and frequency of your interaction with this person? What was the end result? What did you learn from this experience? What would you do differently if you were to do it over again?

Are You Ready For Generation X, Y, or Z?

I hope not. As you hire employees who are perfectly suited to your company, please avoid "fad" thinking at all costs! An example of this kind of thinking is the attempt to differentiate among generations in the workplace.

Certainly, a younger person comes to your business having had digital technology in hand essentially since birth. On the other hand, look at how older generations have adapted to the technology of their times. My grandfather, in 1940, likely drove a car more proficiently than his grandfather did.

In every generation, advancements in industry or technology move society forward. Even so, this is icing on the cake—it is not the cake, itself.

I ignore this flavor-of-the-day thinking and promote a multigenerational and multicultural environment. I feel that employees should be judged based on their values and contributions to the organization. Instead of sorting through manufactured generational nuances, we have learned to focus on the timeless factors that have likely motivated human beings since the beginning. These include:

- Being treated with respect
- Feeling that we matter because our opinions matter
- Being treated and rewarded fairly
- Feeling like a human being, first, and an employee, second
- Being able to see the fruits of our labor

We all recognize these fundamental human needs in our culture. This is a more productive exercise than lamenting about how Generation Y will spell the ruin of the company. Stay away from the fads and let someone else complain meaninglessly. Instead, spend your effort on that which is timeless and universally appreciated.

28

Promoting Accountability with the Perfect Performance Review

A CULTURE OF ACCOUNTABILITY IS essential to your organization's health. As I have discussed, leaders often have difficulty building a true culture of accountability. I want to give you the ultimate weapon with which you can promote accountability. You *must* add "360° reviews" to your arsenal. I realize that these are nothing revolutionary or new, but you might be amazed at how many leaders seem to have difficulty implementing them.

Search the internet for 360° reviews and you will find a confusing amount of data on how to design and execute them. My advice is to keep it simple.

Here are the ground rules I establish prior to embarking on Jetco's annual 360° review process:

The 360° Review

- **Is an opportunity** for peers to provide constructive input regarding the performance of their team members
- **Is an opportunity** for each of us to grow and improve
- **Is an opportunity** to have open and honest discussion, resulting in a more unified team
- **Is NOT** a "guessing game" as to who made what comment
- **Is NOT** an attack
- **Is NOT** to be broadcast to others who are not involved
- **Is NOT** a substitute for the feedback that is required in our everyday interactions

At its core, the 360° review is an effective way for peers to offer valuable insight to one another. Peers see both exemplary and unproductive behavior in a way that is qualitatively different from the way their supervisors do. Here is how I implement the 360° review:

I use a simple plus $(+)$/delta (Δ) form. Employees fill out this form for each member of their review group. They list items that, in their eyes, the reviewed employee should keep doing $(+)$ and items that need to change (Δ).

Once the reviews are complete, I collect and compile the forms, which look something like the following sample:

BOB SMITH 360° Review	
+	**Δ**
+ Tenacity — get it done attitude; follow up + Knows the business; great handle on the pulse of the business + Helpful in passing on knowledge and training; our "go-to" person + Ability to hold yourself together in the middle of chaos + Dedicated; true desire to perform completely. Big progress on measuring production	Δ Strength of conviction can come off as "stand-offish;" let people come to their own solutions; make deliberate effort to listen more in meetings Δ Sometimes needs to catch breath and not show as much emotion Δ Hire the best; don't settle for average. Too quick to defend employees Δ Ask for help; you cannot do it all; delegate!

When collecting the comments, I list frequent/ common items first. It is important to emphasize the most repeated topics so that the recipient of the feedback understands each item's importance as determined by his or her peer group. I limit the +/Δ to about five items each, so that we do not create an unmanageable laundry list.

Once the feedback is compiled, I set up a group meeting (preferably off site) with the members of the peer review group. We present each 360° review with ample time for discussion. While intimidating for first-timers, this process provides a secure forum for employees to provide feedback to one another. My role in the meeting is *not* to provide the feedback or dominate the conversation. Rather, my role is to facilitate the discussion to create a comfortable and respectful environment for a candid conversation.

Throughout the course of the year, I encourage team members to check in with their peers about the topics brought up in their own reviews by asking: "How am I doing?" Ultimately, here is what evolves: The once-difficult and rare feedback in the 360° review becomes a part of our everyday DNA. Once this happens, the 360° review is no longer an annual rite of passage. Rather, it is a way to transform everyday interactions.

Last year, when I was compiling the 360° reviews, I noticed something interesting—many of the themes were often repeated for multiple team members. I isolated these common themes to develop a composite 360° for the team. This is what it looked like:

Did anyone notice… Common themes among our team	
+	Δ
+ Deep knowledge and willing to teach + Passion for customers + Unselfish; works hard + Entrepreneurial + Dedicated — takes ownership	Δ Moody; standoff-ish; abrasive Δ Overly negative when things not going my way; does not assume innocence Δ Prioritize • Involved in too many areas • Take control of your priorities Δ Improve communication Δ Delegate!

This composite review allowed the participants to understand that they were not alone in addressing what they thought were individual challenges. This allowed the team to collectively build on each other's strengths and improve on the most frequently identified weaknesses.

The 360° review is the single most valuable performance review tool I have found to promote accountability. It recognizes that, in a healthy company, feedback comes from all over the organizational chart, recognizing the positive and calling out the negative. Most of all, the 360° review recognizes that in a culture of accountability, feedback is not a one-way street, which helps us to solidify our Three Ts.

My 360° Review: A Look in the Mirror

When it comes to the 360° reviews, let's be clear about one thing: the team at the top should not be exempt from the 360° process. In fact, we can probably benefit from them more than anyone else. With that said, here is the 360° feedback that I received from my team:

360° Feedback from Team	
+	Δ
+ Passion for instilling D2P culture on employees by putting them first; passionate about operating safely. + Empowers employees to make decisions but is available to all. + Fully dedicated and organized on focused growth; long-term thinking at Jetco; great leadership/execution. + Innovative thinker regarding business model. + Technology; marketing — making Jetco "recognized."	Δ Work with us to prioritize projects and tasks. We can only work on so much at a time. Not all opportunities are viable — put our time in best place. Develop better understanding of how long it takes to complete some projects. Δ If Brian and his VP disagree, it can cause changes in process/procedures. Changing again and again until there is agreement is not productive. Δ Lack of appreciation for weekends/time off. We are not all 24/7. Δ Improve office by promoting values — don't accept bad behavior from anyone. Be consistent in enforcement.

Even more than most feedback, this kind of feedback is vital to my development as an effective leader. My 360° review is taped to a wall *at home* to remind me of what I am doing well and what I need to change.

We all need to receive this kind of feedback, but how often does top leadership really receive and learn from it? How well do most of us really receive this level of meaningful input? How did I process this feedback?

First, I thanked everyone for the input. Second, I did not argue with or refute any comments. Third, I committed to reply to the findings with an action plan to build on my strengths and improve that which needed to change. Based on this input, I came to the following conclusions:

- The issue: My mind works 24/7. It is how I am wired. I cannot change that. However, a by-product of this is that I can bombard my team with an unmanageable list of ideas. The solution: I still keep an idea inventory, but I am much more careful to understand each manager's execution list and to not create "idea overload." Furthermore, I am more careful to test ideas before changing course.

- The issue: Over the years, I have come to respect the need for the work-life balance. Those who knew me ten years ago may even think I have become soft! That said, I do not work a traditional schedule. Emails can fly at 4 a.m., or over the weekend. I did not mean to convey an expectation that my team maintain the same hours. Until I received this 360° feedback, I was not aware of the anxiety this was causing. The solution: The 360° review allowed me to clear the air on this topic and reaffirm that, at my company, we measure results—not hours.

The last comment in the Δ column was especially important to me. As you may recall, I do not give myself high marks, at times, in the area of promoting accountability. Well, my team saw the same thing—that I was accepting bad behavior too regularly. In essence, the team gave me license to knock off the "sugar coating" and demand behavior that is in line with our values.

I have always promoted wide-open discussions at our company meetings. I feel that the best results come from disagreement and discussion. However, I have learned that the line must be drawn between healthy debate and a lack of alignment. I found out, through that 360° review, that our team had perceived a disconnect between one of my key executives and me. Based on the feedback I received, it was clear that some of our fierce discussions were better conducted behind closed doors. And, once the debate was over and discussions had been made, I needed to do a better job of promoting alignment and ensuring that we were all marching in the same direction—even if we did not totally agree with the idea.

These are just a few examples of how the 360° process continues to make me a better leader. Like most ideas in this book, implementing this process will result in you spending your time, not your money. This is another very low-cost/high-return activity, and yet it can pave the way for year-round candid communication.

29

Culture-based Compensation

I HAVE BEEN FORTUNATE TO be able to share my D2P story with a number of audiences. I enjoy the act of speaking to groups, but always wish more time was allowed for true dialogue. Instead, most presentations generate email inquiries, and I attempt to reply to each and every one.

I received the following email after one presentation. I think it summarizes the frustration that we all experience when chasing the holy grail of implementing the perfect compensation plan:

From: Paul
Sent: Friday, March 15, 2013 11:18 AM
To: Brian Fielkow
Subject: Attendee Question

Brian, I was very impressed with your presentation at the conference. Most of the industry, including my company, react to problems versus looking for ways to prevent them. I think your D2P program has hit the nail on the head. You said in your introduction that you hoped the audience would take away at least one idea that would help. I'm a firm believer in bonuses. I think they help keep employees focused and give them a prize if they accomplish the set goal.

You mentioned you paid your employees quarterly bonuses in order to keep the "carrot" fairly close. We pay ours annually, but are constantly fighting our employees over taking a substantial bonus cut for a small mistake. I see their point, but what about the employee who makes a big mistake? I can't see paying a quarterly bonus after this kind of loss.

In response to the concerns brought up in that email, I'd like to point out a few steps that I have taken to tie compensation to culture:

No automatic raises: As long as our employees are paid market wages, nobody should expect an automatic raise each year. If we reward our bottom and top performers, we have created the recipe for mediocrity. The same is true for seniority. Why should we reward anyone for longevity if it is not coupled with high performance? I prefer to think about creating raise pools and allocating the pool to my best performers.

No year-end bonuses: Some companies engender a mindset that the year is ending, so they can let the money flow. Too often, bonuses are awarded without a clear tie to the merit or productivity of the employee. In many situations, employees receive bonuses, but do not even know how the amounts were calculated.

Bonuses must be tied to measurable criteria: What good is a profit-based bonus plan if your employees do not know anything about the company's profitability? Employees must understand the ground rules on the first day of the year, and progress must be communicated regularly.

Pay bonuses quarterly: We pay bonuses quarterly. Let's face it; many people in this economy are forced to live from paycheck to paycheck, and quarterly bonuses can make a huge difference to these employees. At the same time, quarterly bonus periods provide the pathway for four reviews per year, which results in better on-going encouragement and feedback.

Rewards must go beyond the individual's contributions: I have used the following bonus plan successfully. The plan accounts for individual performance, team performance, *and* company performance. Without all three of these components working in harmony, bonuses cannot be paid. When you think about it, these components only work in harmony when the company's culture is healthy. In my view, a well-defined bonus plan rewards a healthy culture.

There is no perfect bonus plan, but the following is the best one I have seen. It balances both tangible bonus criteria and necessary management discretion in its implementation.

Sample Bonus Program

Eligible Employees
   To be defined
Target Bonus
   ____% of quarterly base salary

Measurement and Payment Period
Payment will be within 30 days after end of the calendar quarter. An employee can earn up to 100% of his or her bonus target each quarter. Jetco reserves the right, in its discretion, to exceed this target for an employee who delivers truly outstanding results. Employee must be at Jetco for entire calendar quarter to be eligible. Employee is not eligible to participate if he or she is eligible for any other commission or incentive program. For each measurement period, an employee can earn up to 100 points. Based on the employee's score, the employee can earn the following percentages of his/her eligible bonus.

Score	% of Eligible Bonus
95-100	100%
93-96	90%
90-92	85%
85-90	65%
80-85	50%
Below 80	0%

Points will be made available in three (3) categories:

Company Profitability – 20 possible points
In order for this—or any—bonus program to be successful, Jetco must be profitable, meaning that we must meet our budgeted financial goals.

Individual Performance – 40 possible points
Your individual goals will be established and communicated at each quarterly review. These goals will be reviewed with you quarterly and you will receive a quarterly point assignment at that time based on your performance against these goals and your position profile.

Team Performance – 40 possible points
Your team will be judged on overall team performance. We will provide a quarterly scorecard so that you can monitor progress.

People have reviewed this bonus plan and have asked: How can you pay a bonus if the company is not making money? The reply is easy: If our profitability is that bad, a 0/20 financial score eliminates the bonus. More important, however, is the fact that we paid bonuses (albeit small) to our best performers on our best teams all the way through the Great Recession. This goes to prove that an effective bonus plan differentiates between good and bad performers and rewards excellence in all market cycles.

30

Letting Go

MANY BUSINESS AUTHORS ADVISE YOU to continually "pull the weeds" by eliminating your bottom performers, pointing out that this is a tireless, but essential, function. The problem with this advice is that it can ignore *history* and *humanity* as your business exits one stage of its life and enters another.

What do I mean? As a business reaches certain stages of growth, some once-excellent key employees no longer perform at necessary levels. Have they burned out or suddenly given up? Possibly, but not likely. More often than not, the needs of the company have simply outgrown what the employee can contribute. That is where *history* and *humanity* come in.

Let's assume that the employee was vital to your success during a meaningful phase of your company's *history*. Given the employee's contribution, you do not believe it would be *humane* to dismiss or demote the employee. So, what happens? You begin to express frustration with the employee behind closed doors. Then, that frustration escapes closed doors, penetrates the organization, and undermines the employee's ability to perform. Finally, we hire "around" the employee in an effort to bleed away his or her duties and find a confined area for him or her to contribute. This is "death by 1,000 pinpricks" for your employee—and for your company culture.

You and I both know that this happens frequently. It is cruel and unusual punishment levied on a person who was once vital to your success. I wish we could all follow hardnosed business guidance—"that's the way the world works, fire the poor performer and move on." Unfortunately, many of us do not work that way. I have been confronted with this situation in my own career, and the following plan of action has worked for me:

- Have an open and honest discussion with the employee. Let him or her know your assessment of the situation. If you have concluded that the situation is beyond repair, let the employee know. Do not hold out hope when there is none.
- Listen for options. Even before you have to make any pronouncements, the employee may express a sigh of relief. Chances are that your employee knows that the train has left the station.
- Solutions will present themselves. First, ask yourself what qualities made this employee a great contributor. Perhaps there is a role in your company that will leverage those strengths, into which the employee could move. For example, a wayward general operations manager may be happier managing a smaller division.

- Be prepared for some push-back. In many cases, the employee is not likely to accept what is perceived to be a demotion. Outwardly, he or she may tell you that this is acceptable, but it is more likely that he or she is buying time. The employee may fear embarrassment caused by accepting a lower position.
- Finally, be prepared to cut the cord. A clean break is often the best. A generous severance package may be acceptable to thank the employee for his or her contribution and secure an orderly transition— and should be open for discussion. Then, you and your employee will both be free to explore greener pastures.

No matter what the outcome, if you stay true to your company's culture and values—and don't short-change either yourself or your employee—you will know that you've done the right thing. Letting any employee go is never easy, but you'll be able to sleep easier if you do it with both history and humanity in mind.

PART VI:

CULTURE KILLERS

31

Growth Can
Kill Your Culture

NORMALLY, WE LOOK AT GROWTH as positive. However, if your company grows too fast or haphazardly and without sufficient planning and infrastructure, your values can become vulnerable to compromise. You run the risk of involuntarily losing control of your company's greatest asset: its culture. As leaders, we must push our companies beyond their boundaries toward profitable growth. However, we must also control the growth—and not allow the growth to control us.

I learned this lesson while I was COO of a Midwestern recycling company. We had grown organically with great success and determined that it was time for us to grow by acquisition. We identified what seemed to be a perfect target. All of the boxes were checked: long-standing company, respectable market share, desirable market, an owner who was willing to transition, and tangible synergies.

During due diligence, we failed to recognize the massive cultural gap between our two companies. In particu-

lar, integrity was very important to us. In the recycling industry, some competitors paid a high price for recyclables—but
on a fraction of the actual weight. We paid a fair price on real
weight. Integrity was one of our core values.

We learned, too late, that our target company had
the weight game down to a science. The company's management fooled their customers—and us. I consider this to be
one of the greatest mistakes I have made. I didn't pick up
on this cultural disconnect because I was too busy verifying
customer information and operating metrics to really understand what was happening right under my nose.

We thought that we could fix the problem, but we
could not—the value gap was too large. We hopelessly cycled
our team members into the operation to insert our business
practices, but to no avail. Customer perceptions eroded when
we began to pay them a fair (albeit lower) price per ton on
real weights.

The business never moved beyond breaking even. In
reality, it was a huge loss in terms of the human capital which
we had to spend on attempting to fix an irreparable cultural gap.

You do not need a negative acquisition experience to
undermine the culture you are building. Poor hiring practices
will land you in the same undesirable spot. It is essential that
you hire for culture and aptitude above all else. Of course,
while saying that, I am not downplaying the importance of
job-specific skills. If you need a CPA, you need to hire a CPA.
Even so, when you advertise for the position, you will find
that there are many well-trained CPAs, but a relatively small
number of them will fit your culture.

If you hire for skill but ignore culture, every new
employee represents a risk to your culture. The best way to
determine if there is a cultural fit is to carefully develop a

series of questions to test the candidates' alignment with your values. For instance, I like to know how candidates perceive and address integrity issues, how they handle conflict with co-workers, and how they have handled seemingly insurmountable challenges. I prefer to have a team of several people interview each candidate to get the best possible assessment of their possible cultural fit.

Over the years, I have learned that not all growth is good, whether in the form of an acquisition or in the form of bringing a new person into my culture. I learned that it is vitally important to ensure that any growth opportunity will enhance and further my own company's valuable culture. Finally, I have learned to *never* underestimate the difficulty (if not the impossibility) of repairing or changing cultures that are fundamentally out of sync with mine.

A Better Way to Think About Growth

Ever since the beginning of our business careers, we have been exposed to certain conventional wisdom: "Growth is good. If you are not going forward, you are going backward. Grow or die."

Certainly, we desire healthy, profitable growth. However, many of us make growth the goal in our business. I have learned to view growth a little differently: Growth happens when you execute with purpose and excellence. Growth is not a goal—it is the end product of a job well done.

I have seen too many people compromise their careers in pursuit of some broad-minded growth target. Invariably, managers will stretch to hit these growth goals, and the road is littered with the end results, which might include:

- Failed acquisitions;
- Unprofitable top line revenue; and
- Ill-timed diversification that compromises the core business.

I have learned to pursue excellence in all aspects of my business. When I have executed my plans properly, growth has resulted. Because I have faith in my company and our culture, I do not lie awake worried that we missed some artificially fabricated target. On the other hand, if I detect problems in our culture or with D2P-led execution, I am highly concerned. In that case, growth will certainly suffer.

Even the process of raising capital can change your culture. Private investors could limit how you deploy capital. Investors also require an exit in a defined period of time (i.e. five to seven years). What if the exit coincides with a significant business opportunity or downturn? Pushed to its extreme, the exit could trigger a sale of the company—not exactly the intended outcome if you're trying to drive growth.

As you raise capital to pursue a new growth spurt, consider whether any of the terms and conditions will affect your ability to control your company, culture, and ultimate destiny. There is not a "right" or "wrong" decision. Instead, I am simply encouraging you to consider the potential impact on your culture and destiny that a fundamental transaction, such as raising capital, may present.

My attitude toward profitable growth changed dramatically as soon as I learned to enjoy the pursuit of excellence and to recognize that growth is simply a by-product of a successful journey. I no longer choose growth at all costs, having realized that the wrong kind of growth can cause unwanted and unneeded overhead, complexity, and infrastructure—all of which ultimately detract from running a truly excellent business.

32

Buyer Beware

IF YOU SET OUT TO acquire a company, remember the old adage "buyer beware." I suggest that this maxim does not apply to the actions of the seller, however; it applies to your own actions as a buyer. I have seen sellers destroy very few acquisitions. In contrast, *buyers* destroy countless deals, and I never used to understand why.

If you think about it, the seller has limited ways to blow your deal. The seller may misrepresent the product or mislead the buyer. The seller may violate a non-compete clause in a contract or otherwise commit acts of sabotage. Beyond that, however, the buyer bears responsibility for most failed acquisitions.

The buyer might blow up a deal at the front end because he or she overpaid, made faulty assumptions about the purchase, or did not perform proper due diligence. These are common errors that the buyer can—and should—evaluate and correct the next time an acquisition is proposed.

The more significant and insidious issue facing buyers is a simple failure to plan for the integration of the combined businesses. We become so focused on the steps leading up to the closing of the deal that integrating the current holdings with the new one becomes an afterthought.

What are we integrating when we acquire a new company? People and process, or—in other words—culture. If you think everything is fine at the outset, but find out that the combined cultures do not fit *post*-closing, it is too late for you to do anything about it.

In Chapter 31, I discussed how our failure to focus on culture and values caused terrible results for us when we tried to combine two recycling businesses with very different cultures. When I bought my current business, I did not make the same mistake. After getting through the basics, I spent my time with the company's founder and its employees. Before making any decisions, I insisted on meeting with some of the customers and vendors, as well.

Through my due diligence, I was able to develop a picture in my mind of what I was buying and the value that I could create. An outsider, having not done research, might have seen an owner nearing retirement and could have drawn conclusions that the business was either broken or tired. I saw the opposite. I saw a group of extremely hard-working people who had started a business with one truck in 1976 and who had come to the realization that they needed to change.

While we were from different backgrounds, I could tell that this company and I shared the same set of values: hard work and dedication, passion for customer service, and a refusal to compete solely on price.

I knew that I would need to make changes in order to bring the company to the next level. I could tell from the outset that these changes would involve people, process, technology, capital, and culture. I recognized that change would take a long time and that I would encounter resistance, but I was prepared to accept this challenge because I had done my homework on the company's culture and concluded that the values were lined up properly. No amount of financial, legal, or operational due diligence could have resulted in me knowing so much about what I was getting into.

I am proud that many of Jetco's original employees, including two of the previous owners, still work with me today. As a result, we were able to capture everything that made the company successful from 1976 until I took over in 2006, as we paved the way for the next 30 years.

33

Values vs. Priorities— Know the Difference

THERE WILL BE NO GREATER test of your company's commitment to its core values than a customer conflict. Since the beginning of our careers, we all have been taught that if a customer tells us to jump, we should ask "How high?" I believe that, instead, we should be asking "Why?" and whether this aligns with our value system and our ability to deliver long-term value for our customers.

Knowing the difference between *values* and *priorities* is often the single greatest point of confusion for an organization. Values define us and bind us together, drive decisions in all of our interactions, and never change. Priorities, on the other hand, are tasks requiring action, must be managed daily, and shift frequently based on a given situation. But, even though priorities are the starting points for your day-to-day activities, your values should always guide your actions. Understand that people often do not properly differentiate values from priorities. You must ensure that broad-based understanding exists within your company, and that—while your priorities may shift—your values are never compromised.

Values vs. Priorities

Values
- Define who we are and bind us together
- Are defined in every interaction—including those with coworkers, customers, and the public

Priorities
- Things that need to get done
- Can and do change

Although priorities may vary from person to person and from day to day, on a winning team everyone has knowledge of—and is committed to—the same values.

For example, safety is a core value at my company. We priced a project for one of our customers to include transportation permits and police escorts due to the large and operationally challenging nature of the cargo. Our competitor did not include the same safeguards in their pricing. As a result, our bid—at face value—was more expensive and at a price disadvantage. In fact, our customer was angered by our pricing. They challenged us to bid the project at the same low cost as our competitor, even "reminding us" that they spend a lot of money with our company.

The message was clear: the account was at risk. To be sure, we had a few sleepless nights wrestling with the short-term implications of the situation. We struggled, knowing the project's safety risks were low. We wondered whether we really needed all of the safety precautions, or whether we should simply follow our competitor's less-rigorous lead.

Even though, from an outside viewpoint, our top priority probably should have been the money, in the end, we stuck to our values. We were prepared to risk losing the business to keep our unwavering commitment to our values. In the end, a cultural breakdown was avoided, and we also stayed off the slippery slope which would no doubt have come from the resulting safety lapses certain to occur once we no longer remained focused on safety as one of our top values.

Looking back on the situation, the only logical conclusion is that no piece of business is worth compromising the values that drive sound business practices. There is enough risk when you execute your business in the right way, and there is no reason to ask for problems if you don't need them. Let's say an accident had occurred. Would *the customer* have paid for the accident? Would *their* reputation have suffered? Or would all of the bad press focused on us?

I'm happy to say that, as strange as it seems, even after all of the difficult discussions with our customer, we kept the business and won the bid. Our values remained intact, and the customer gained more respect for us because we did what was right, not what was convenient.

Without question, a company that blindly follows a customer-first mentality will destroy any ability to build a truly excellent, value-driven company. "The customer is always right" is simply management code for "I don't care what needs to be done, just get it done." This creates an environment that is focused on fighting fires throughout the organization, rather than taking the time to empower employees based on a common culture of shared values and a vision designed to ensure that the right decisions are made the first time. Without a consistently articulated culture, you may succeed financially and enjoy profitability, but you likely are missing opportunities, hurting morale, and inviting more risk than you can handle down the road.

It is our responsibility, as leaders, to ensure that our teams know the difference between values and priorities and to ensure that those values are never compromised. Here are a few tips to keep in mind as you align your values with your customers' demands:

- Customer concentration ratios are key. If a single customer accounts for a disproportionate share of your revenue, are you more likely to compromise your values to accommodate that customer and avoid losing business? Is this healthy for the culture of your business?

- All business is good, but not all business is good to have. Each business must have a means to identify and recognize customers who fit well with its product and service offering. A well-articulated value package allows you to identify appropriately matched customers. For example, a customer who only focuses on price may never appreciate your particular quality-driven value proposition.

- Some customers you can train, some you cannot. If you feel you are spending eighty percent of your time fixing problems associated with twenty percent of your customers, look more closely at the situation.

Some customers in that twenty percent simply may not fit your company's core strengths. These will probably turn out to be the same customers who continually negotiate every last nickel, even after the service is performed. Granted, some of these customers can be "trained." Your company may simply have failed to convincingly articulate what makes you different from other companies. Once these customers realize what drives you, they may readily embrace your value proposition. But other customers are not trainable. The faster you appreciate the difference, the quicker you will recognize and replace the time-bandit customers and focus your effort on more profitable endeavors.

- Buy their business and you buy a problem. Beware of customers who perpetually seek to have their palms greased. If you get their business because you give them tickets to an event in the tenth row, you will easily lose their business to a competitor who offers them row nine. Invariably, you risk your own standing in the eyes of valuable customers or prospects simply because you choose to compete on the level of arbitrary factors, rather than competing on the strength of what you can offer.

- Successful businesses cultivate relationships. Trust develops through the relationship-building process. There is no substitute for building a solid business relationship. Through this process, your customer will better understand your values and will think before asking you to violate your values.

Always pay attention to the fact that a single overly demanding customer—who is not kept in check by those in the executive office—could destroy your entire team. Customers with consistently unrealistic demands create an opportunity for conflict between leadership and employees when they begin to push your priorities out of line from your values. You need to remember that your employees are smart. They will work tirelessly for a leader who has their back and supports a consistent, value-based culture. Conversely, they will reject a leader who continually sets them up to fail, simply because he does not have the backbone to properly manage customer expectations and lets changing priorities dictate the business.

34

Complacency and Your Culture

I HAVE DISCUSSED HOW WELL-intentioned, but ill-conceived, growth can consume your culture. Now let's address complacency—it will kill your culture faster than anything outside force. Here are a few signs that complacency may be taking root in your company:

- You have had a string of success. You get the sense that people are pretty proud of themselves and have become enamored with their own success.
- The process is relaxed, in favor of just getting the job done.
- Some of your employees have decided that "good" is "good enough," and you no longer see their unrelenting quest for continuous improvement.

As leaders, one of our most important functions we can fulfill is to look for early signs of complacency and drive them out of the organization, even if that means driving some people out along with it. Let me give you an example:

> The time came for a routine government compliance review. My philosophy has always been that we must be ready for audits anytime, anywhere, and without notice, but this time I recognized that there was some discomfort and concern about the pending audit from my compliance team.
>
> After digging, I realized that this was because our files were not in optimal shape for the audit. Fortunately, we had everything we needed, but it took a lot of work to make the files "audit ready."
>
> This lack of readiness hit me like a ton of bricks. Complacency had crept in. Our safety record had made us a less-likely candidate for an audit, so we hadn't worried about keeping our files in shape. When our time came, we had let our guard down and were simply not ready.

Unchecked, this "we don't need to worry" attitude can and will infiltrate your company. If it does not infiltrate your whole company, it will creep into departments. Unfortunately, until something big happens, complacency will not be obvious to you unless you are looking for it. So, how do you identify complacency and drive it out of your company? There is no single answer. In most cases, the solution will be something tailored to your specific organization, but these ideas have worked for me and can be guidelines for your company, as well:

Audits: Whether you decide to conduct these internally or by using outside sources, you should develop an audit process to ensure that your policies and procedures are being followed. No matter how much faith you have in your team, the audit process is necessary to keep everyone on their toes, and you must be willing to create a certain level of discomfort—although anyone who is truly working at 100% won't have to worry.

Develop your own antenna: Once you've worked with the same team for a while, you'll find that your instinct is rarely wrong for what is and isn't working. Look for a handful of items that you can look at regularly to determine if something is off track. In my business, my barometer is a mix of safety issues and measuring at-fault service failures. In a previous position, my boss's barometer was housekeeping of the production facilities—if the corners were dirty, he knew that deeper issues existed.

No excuses/No explanations: When faced with challenges, determine if your team is geared to fix the problem or simply justify it with excuses. For example, driver recruitment is an ongoing challenge in my industry. To make things more difficult, we have high hiring standards. When recruiting slows down, I may receive excuses like: "Brian, remember . . . we are fishing from a small pond. There are not a lot of candidates who meet our standards." When this type of excuse is presented, I simply remind the team that the pond cannot be that small in the fourth largest market in the country. Moreover, if we really live up to our headlines, should we not be a magnet for attracting the best?

Unchecked, excuses can infiltrate your company and become a justification for complacency and, ultimately, failure. The faster you stop accepting excuses, the faster you will kill complacency. Excuses are wrapped in many different packages that might include:

- I am too busy.
- My predecessor left a mess for me.
- I didn't have the resources.

And the list goes on. The minute you buy into any excuses, you have joined the bandwagon. You are enabling excuses and, ultimately, complacency.

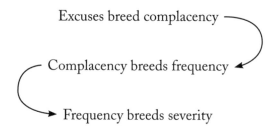

Excuses breed complacency

Complacency breeds frequency

Frequency breeds severity

Part of building a vibrant and sustainable culture requires you, as a leader, to keep complacency in check. This is a tireless function. If you take your eye off the ball for even a short time, complacency *will* find its way into your organization.

35

Killing Complacency with Communication

COMPLACENCY IS THE BIGGEST THREAT to excellence. No question about it. How does a high-performing team become complacent? Does everyone wake up one day and decide to check out? Complacency is not a cause, but an end product—the effect of something going wrong in your culture. In my organization, I have noticed that complacency results most commonly from these situations:

Lack of focus—When there are too many competing demands even good managers become paralyzed. They transform from proactive leaders into reactive firefighters. Eventually, they stop caring about the big picture.

Lack of clarity—In this case, team leaders receive conflicting and confusing instructions from one or more senior managers (or front-line staff might receive from their supervisors). Lack of clarity creates insecurity and frustration. It causes good people to check out.

Lack of purpose—Without a sense of purpose, employees do not understand the company's core mission or their vital role in its success. They drift. Processes are not followed, and people fill the void with their own agendas. No one is looking out for the greater good.

As leaders, driving complacency out of our organization is one of our most important functions. Simple and repeated communication can kill complacency. Here is what works for me:

- We create simple, personal, and understandable messages. We communicate them often and ensure they are consistent. We have learned that, if you do not communicate, a lack of trust will grow. If you communicate sporadically or give confusing/contradictory messages, confusion will paralyze the team. On the other hand, clear, consistent communication creates a sense of purpose.
- Every employee participates in a bi-weekly meeting. Each meeting is focused on a different topic, but all topics are centered on our values and mission. The meetings are participatory, not simply lectures. This ensures that the management team sees every employee twenty-six times per year. This is a challenge for an industry where the majority of our employees are generally in the field, but we feel it is time well spent in giving everyone a clear sense of our company's values.
- We send a letter to our employees' homes monthly. We want our "extended family" to know what is going on at the company and to understand the level of care we have for each employee. Without questions coming from their families, it is easier for our employees to remain focused at work.

- We have fun. Not everything has to be serious. At a recent company celebration, we hired a standup comedian to entertain our team. The celebration drove pride and underscored each employee's role in our mission. This kind of non-work activity develops an emotional connection to the company, which instills a sense of purpose in everyone.

Not long ago, we held a competition asking our employees what "Driving to Perfection" means to them. The following was written by the *spouse* of an employee. There is true passion in these words.

WHAT DOES D2P MEAN TO YOU?

Since September 2010, we've been on the road to perfection by following the values and behaviors of Driving 2 Perfection. We want to know, what does D2P mean to you?

Here's what D2P means to me: DRIVING TO PERFECTION MEANS CARING ABOUT OTHERS, THAT MOTHER ON HER WAY TO WORK AFTER DROPPING OFF HER 2 KIDS. THE SON THAT ASPIRES TO BE A DOCTOR WHO WILL ONE DAY FIND THE CURE FOR CANCER. THE GRANDPA WHOS GRANDAUGHTER CANT WAIT TO SEE SO HE CAN TELL HER AGAIN ABOUT HIS EXPERIENCES AROUND THE WORLD. IT'S ABOUT FAMILY & LOVE. BE SAFE! YOU NEVER KNOW HO IS IN THE CAR NEXT TO YOU!

The author of that note had never been to our training sessions, and yet she knew all about our company's values and ideals. Her words, along with those in many similar submissions, assured me that we have been driving our message successfully to our team members' families.

All of our communications are designed to reinforce focus, clarity, and sense of purpose. Because people learn and respond differently, we use different modes of communication including:

- Email blasts;
- Voicemail blasts;
- Memos;
- Letter to employees' homes;
- Meetings;
- One-on-one discussions; and
- Videos.

Some may say that our communication is repetitious, but not every communication is centered on the next greatest idea. Instead, they repeat and reinforce our core values and objectives, driving out complacency along the way.

36

Progressive Discipline

SINCE THE BEGINNING OF OUR careers, we have been taught that progressive discipline is the necessary way to reprimand or rehabilitate wayward employees. In the classic discipline structure, the employee first receives a written warning to correct his or her behavior. On the next offense, the employee receives a second written warning; then perhaps another written warning is issued, followed by termination.

In my opinion, classic progressive discipline must be retired. The process was born out of the need to protect a company in case of a wrongful termination lawsuit. However, it is a backward way to approach our employees—especially when corrective action is necessary.

The first problem with progressive discipline is that it robs our managers of their judgment. If all incidents are processed in the same way, how do we distinguish between severe and minor infractions? How do we distinguish between an employee who has three strikes over five years, compared to an individual with three strikes in his or her first year?

The second problem with progressive discipline is that it drains the employee's morale and commitment to the company. If the employee is on her second strike, she might already be dusting off her resume as opposed to meaningfully engaging in ways to improve performance.

Finally, let's admit it—managers work around progressive discipline every day. In some cases, incidents are not documented to avoid triggering a "strike." Some employees are allowed to have more strikes than the policy permits.

Obviously, traditional progressive discipline is good for neither the employee nor the supervisor. Instead, consider a coaching process where the employee and his or her supervisor can discuss the incident *and* a performance improvement plan. This shift from progressive discipline to coaching will improve morale and increase employee alignment around acceptable behaviors. Through coaching, you should also be able to retain salvageable employees and build them into solid contributors. Compare this to the cost of terminating and replacing an employee with someone you do not know, and you can immediately see its benefits.

While you can guess that I prefer the coaching and training suggested by a rich culture, none of this is to suggest that I favor a soft approach to discipline. Based on the frequency and severity of offenses, there are times when an aggressive approach to addressing challenging employees (including, as a last choice, termination of the employee) is warranted. That said, in many cases you will achieve a much better interim result through coaching your employee as opposed to being adversarial.

Of course, this leaves open the question of legal protections. I suggest you design an employee development system that fits your culture, then review it with your attorney to ensure adequate protection. You'll quickly find that this is preferable to having a cookie-cutter, progressive discipline policy thrust upon your company which is not in sync with your culture or your values.

Contrast how a rich culture and poor culture might each handle the same challenges:

Pick a problem... any problem: • Quality • Safety • Sales You name it!	Poor Culture	Rich Culture
	• Blame the employees. • Hire more management. Create greater levels of control. Build the bureaucracy. • Develop more compliance requirements and paperwork. • Send messages such as: "Fix the problem or you're fired."	• Create a multi-level, multi-disciplinary team to develop structural solutions. • Move from crisis management mentality to culture of prevention. Empowered employees will get in front of the problem. • On-going training programs provide employees with the knowledge and tools to make the right decisions. • The front-line management is accountable. Other departments support the efforts of the front-line.

37

Tear Down the Silos

SILOS WILL KILL YOUR CULTURE. Make no mistake about it. As we briefly discussed earlier in Chapter 3, silos are self-imposed barriers which exist among various divisions or departments of your company. Where silos exist, look for this type of dialogue:

> *"Quality is suffering. That is the problem of the manufacturing or engineering department."*—Even though the sales team may be able to pinpoint exactly where the problem exists from the customers' perspective.

> *"We are having too many accidents. Call the safety director."*—Even though the safety director cannot prevent accidents as effectively as the front-line operations staff.

> *"Our employee turnover is too high. See what HR can do to fix the problem."*—Even though HR contact

with employees is only a fraction of the amount of contact which goes on between the employees and their managers.

If it is so obvious that a silo-based company cannot achieve excellence, why are silos continually erected? Basically, some employees will gravitate to what is in their sphere of control or expertise and then keep everyone else out of that sphere. When a few of them band together in this mindset, the silo immediately takes shape.

This game of passing the buck—or simply avoiding "the buck" completely—happens in my organization, and I trust you have experienced it, as well. To compound the problem, the people creating the silos are often our managers.

If your managers allow silos to arise, you could have a real problem. One group of employees may be sitting on the sidelines watching another group struggle—or fail. Few silo dwellers are truly concerned about the greater good of the enterprise—they typically worry only about their own narrow area.

Ultimately, then, the buck needs to stop with the leaders. Silos only grow if leadership allows them to. One of our most important functions as leaders is to create an environment of *inter*dependence. I recognize that simple business organization requires the creation of departments. It is not practical to operate as one undefined mass with no rhyme or reason or chain of command. That said, the need for divisions does not mean that silos are inevitable.

So, how do we as leaders tear down these silos? There is no silver bullet, and the process may involve some trial and error. Even so, here are a few ideas that have worked for me:

- Design your meetings to be cross-functional. For example, ensure that a finance and operations manager participates in sales meetings. The scope and agenda of the meeting can be focused, but the people around the table should represent a broader constituency of the company.

- Ensure that your system of recognition, reward, and advancement benefits employees whose behavior promotes the greater good of the entire organization. This may be a leader who builds cross-functional teamwork. It also may be a front-line employee who identifies a process improvement that will benefit the whole company.

- Create clarity so that your organization knows what you expect. Silos form the easiest when there is a void. The first walls are built when no one is looking. As a leader, you are in the best position to repetitively communicate and reinforce the behaviors that are required for company success, and to continually tear down those walls before they grow.

- Above all, remind your entire company that you are all working together to achieve your goals, that you all share the same values, and that you couldn't move forward without each and every department.

My company actually consists of four interdependent business units. A few years ago, I began to see a different type of silo form—one that exposed a division between our office personnel and our drivers. To tear down this silo, we asked our drivers to elect a committee of their peers. We empowered this committee to be involved in all aspects of life at our company. That committee has direct input on pay, company policy, work environment, and more. Most importantly, our office team looks to this committee for guidance, as well as feedback from our overall team of drivers. This committee has become the link needed to create better alignment between two equally important groups of employees.

We've made sure to drive this message home to our employees by communicating our goals and ideals—and cross-company praise—directly to them. As with anything else, we believe that trust and transparency can help break down silo walls, too.

What aspects of your company could you put into a letter to your employees?

Dear Jetco Team:

Welcome to a new year! As we continue our drive to perfection, I ask you to remember this:

- We could not service our customers without our safe, professional drivers.
- Our drivers could not run without a shop staff that works tirelessly to keep our equipment in excellent repair.
- Our shop would not be able to obtain the parts and supplies needed to service our drivers without the finance team collecting receivables and paying our bills on time or ahead of schedule and managing our resources carefully.
- Our finance team would not have the cash to pay our bills without world-class sales and marketing efforts.
- Our sales team could not keep our customers "begging for more" without our committed operations and customer service teams, who are always working to exceed expectations.
- Without our safety, compliance, and technology teams, our operations team would not have the tools and information to keep running safely and efficiently in accordance with our D2P values.
- Let's begin this year with thanks and gratitude for each other and the contribution that each of us makes to our great team. I can honestly say that I have never worked with a more passionate or committed group of professionals. Never forget—we need each other!

Brian

PART VII:

MEASURING CULTURE

38

Measuring Culture from the Outside

IF I HAVE CONVINCED YOU that building a vibrant company culture is the single most important investment that you can make, then it is fair for you to ask whether there is a return on that investment. Let me assure you that the return is clear. You will see it in areas such as employee morale and productivity—and customer relationships.

I wanted to test whether our customers actually understood and appreciated our culture, so I engaged the Customer Manufacturing Group (CMG) to perform a customer survey. I did this because of their wholly unique survey method. Instead of a strict, metric-based survey, they were focused on qualitative factors. CMG engaged in thirty- to sixty-minute conversations with our customers. This provided me with meaningful data to determine if our culture was, in fact, making an impact on our customers.

The following is an unedited summary of the overall findings.

Jetco is considered to be a first-class, highly regarded, top-rated company. Some customers view you as the industry "gold standard" or "best-in-class" operation in some aspects of your service, and many of these in the combination of service, performance, communications, and people. Jetco is becoming, and already is for a few customers, a prime example of what a very top company should look like.

No customer indicated that he/she believed that Jetco was becoming complacent in attitude, service, or performance. In fact, when the interviewer asked each survey participant what Jetco would have to do in order to be considered a "great company," many respondents replied, "they already are."

The report section titled "The Voice of Your Customers" provides more detail of what value(s) your customers consider to be your hallmarks of performance excellence, but as an overall topic banner, Jetco's "customer service" in all of its various aspects garnered the most frequently stated positive attribute.

Specifically, Jetco's entire cadre of customer-facing service providers, regardless of what service each provided, was rated one of the best, if not the best, in the asset-based trucking industry. It wasn't just the quality of some business and/or technical service, but the posi-

*tive, friendly, extra-mile attitude with which
the service was provided. Your customers enjoy
working with you (and in CMG's experience,
very few companies have achieved this accolade).*

I did not expect to receive such glowing feedback
from a blind survey process. I had simply been testing for
the connection between our culture and our customers. Had
we adopted a "customer-first at any price" policy, I doubt
we would have seen these results. Instead, we focus on our
employees first, and, therefore, they are trained and empowered to take care of the customer. It is why customers enjoy
working with us and why they come back, day after day, with
repeat business.

Still not convinced? Does this sound like I am simply
offering you "feel good" language? Then, let me provide you
with some hard numbers. Much of our growth is defined by
expanding the existing customers' "share of the wallet." This
means that we seek to capture more of our customers' freight
spending from year to year. Here are the results from our top
fifteen customers:

Customer	As of December 31				
	Year 1	Year 2	Year 3	Year 4	Year 5
1	$419	$587	$1,456	$1,923	$2,840
2	337	780	1,374	1,365	2,396
3	10	273	398	684	1,388
4	900	977	1,004	1,182	1,043
5	124	37	91	420	954
6	7	19	111	499	844
7	255	429	729	795	815
8	331	197	203	431	642
9	1,270	606	376	565	518
10	9	9	2	22	454
11	156	65	114	433	432
12	-	16	261	397	415
13	131	106	242	278	384
14	351	177	690	427	365
15	-	-	-	2	333

Dollar amounts are in thousands.

We would not have achieved anywhere near these results had we not developed a meaningful, unique customer experience that was grounded in a value-driven culture. Specifically, our employees are empowered to provide an excellent customer experience based in the values we all hold important to us, and are given the tools and training to accomplish this.

Of course, how you measure culture really depends on the metrics that are of greatest importance to your business. Great customer service and company growth can only evolve from a strong culture of empowerment. However, if you had any doubts, the chart above should prove to you that building a rich, solid culture is a positive investment of time *with a measurable return.*

39

Measuring Culture
from the Inside

ANOTHER EXCELLENT WAY TO MEASURE the benefits of your company's culture is to survey your employees. For the survey to be effective, avoid closed-ended questions or any answer on a one-to-ten scale. Instead, ask open-ended questions that must be measured qualitatively.

If your specialized survey does not meet someone else's scientific metrics, it's no big deal. You are seeking actionable responses, not simply data you can put on a graph. Here is a sample of the questions, and most common replies, that we have asked and received:

The things I like most about my job are:

- I am free to do the job my way, as long as I stay within company policy.
- The family bond that this company shows toward its employees.
- I love the safety culture.

The company could help me be better by:

- Communicating more.
- Creating opportunity for advancement.
- Listening to the employees more.

Feedback like this is worth its weight in gold. As leaders, we must mine for this gold. Once it is in our hands, it is an opportunity for us to build on our strengths and improve on our weaknesses.

The replies show that our employees recognize and appreciate our culture, but that we have room to improve. We know that our company culture is not for everyone, and those who are not in alignment will not last long at our company. But those who embrace the culture will have a long-term home at our company.

As you do an internal review of areas in need of improvement within your own company, it is essential that you act accordingly. These areas for improvement cannot be ignored. For example:

- When we learned that our employees felt they weren't hearing all that was going on, we improved communication in a number of ways, including frequent listening sessions, home mailings, and daily emails.
- In response to the criticism that we had not created a clear path for advancement, we defined a program called the "5 levels." Each level involves a defined set of skills and competencies. Employees have the opportunity to advance from one level to the next through a defined process. This allows our employees to continually grow in terms of career satisfaction

and to be rewarded appropriately. Before we implemented the "5 levels," it was not clear to employees how they could advance in the company. Now, the control is in the employee's hands. He or she knows the skills, training, and time needed to advance. It is up to him or her to come forward and request progression. Once we have been informed of that desire, we will invest the time and effort in this progression. This is much better than "black box" advancement, which leaves some employees feeling left behind.

In both of these examples, listening to our employees made us better. We were able to advance our culture to a new level because we measured the alignment of our employees to our culture.

Are these qualitative measurements too soft for you? If so, you can also measure the effectiveness of your internal culture with hard data. We engaged an outside firm to poll our employees and plot their perceptions of our company's successes against a standardized benchmark for our industry Here is a sample of what we found:

Factors

The black bars on this chart show Jetco Delivery's average score on each factor. The gray bars provide the average score on each factor for the "Distribution, Logistics & Freight – 2012" benchmark.

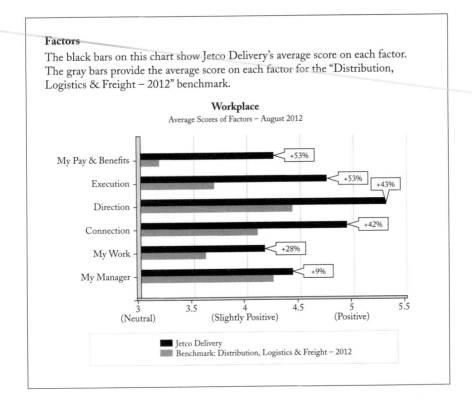

Workplace
Average Scores of Factors – August 2012

You can see that we are outperforming the industry benchmark in each of the surveyed areas. You can also see that our employees' perceptions about their managers were close to average—not negative, but not much more positive than the norm—so that is something we need to look at if we want to drive for excellence. Combining this data with what we learned from our internal surveys allows us to focus our training and development resources on the items which are generating the lowest scores.

When gathering data, it is helpful to measure employees' cultural alignment by asking the same questions at repetitive intervals. In Chapter 10, I listed sample questions to test for cultural alignment and internal stakeholder perceptions. When we first asked these questions in 2010, we found a number of disconnects between our rosy perception and a more disjointed reality.

We administered the exact same set of questions to our team three years later, and we found the following:

- Over 90% of the respondents viewed safety as their #1 priority.
- 91% of the respondents expressed great pride in our brand and in being part of the company.
- 89% of the respondents knew what was expected of them and would recommend our company as a good place to work. In fact, many of our best new hires came from employee referrals.

By asking the same questions at defined intervals, we are able to determine if we are moving forward at the desired pace. By measuring our cultural progress, we also recognize that our journey never ends. If we become complacent, our scores are certain to deteriorate.

Performing periodic pressure checks helps our culture evolve. What worked for today will not likely work for tomorrow, and that is what keeps each day of the journey fresh and exciting. It is what keeps me, as a business leader, coming back for more.

Clearly, you must decide what metrics work for your own organization. But, with a little thought—and possibly some outside help—you'll find that culture is tangible and measurable if you simply define and measure it against the benchmarks that are most important to you.

40

Wrapping It Up

IN WRITING THIS BOOK, I have attempted to give you practical and usable ideas that require your time—but not excessive amounts of money. In that spirit, the following is a brief summary of what we have learned as we have built our culture at Jetco.

What have we learned about building culture?

- Perfection is the only acceptable goal . . . period!
- Never confuse priorities for values.
- You can't *manage* it if you can't *measure* it; you *can* measure cultural success.
- Positive culture is all about attitude.

- Manage behavior and the results will come.
- Communicate the victories *and* the setbacks.
- Vigorously protect your culture.
- Confront behavior that is out of line with your values.
- Ensure that people who do not share your values are not on your team.
- True accountability happens at the "peer-to-peer" level.

As the years slip by, I have come to terms with how short our lives and careers are. In the past, I have thought that when I retired perhaps I would volunteer to help people. However, I have no guarantee that I will have that ability when I retire. In fact, there is no guarantee that any of us will make it to retirement.

That said, each of us has the opportunity to make a difference in the lives of others—now. By running the best possible company, you are enhancing the lives of your employees *and* of your customers. The minute any of us becomes indifferent to our calling as a leader, it truly will be time to find something different to do.

We live in a world of unlimited opportunities. The only limitations we have are those we impose upon ourselves. Building a great culture requires passion, drive, and an uncompromising commitment to excellence.

I truly hope that I was able to share a few ideas that will help your company progress to a whole new level. It is a great honor for me to know that you took the time to read this book. I thank you for your valuable time.

I wish you all the best as you **DRIVE TO PERFECTION!**

PART VIII:

ADDITIONAL
REFERENCES

Additional References

I AM OFTEN ASKED ABOUT my favorite business books. The ones I appreciate the most are those which I have read many times over. Here is my short list:

Carnegie, Dale. *How to Stop Worrying and Start Living.* New York: Simon and Schuster, 1948.

This book is intimately personal. It addresses how we must handle our fears and worries. While seven decades old, this book continues to be timely and relevant, proving that it is impossible to manage change if you are paralyzed with worry.

Bossidy, Larry. *Execution: The Discipline of Getting Things Done.* New York: Crown Business, 2002.

I enjoy this book because of its central argument that businesspeople are bombarded with great ideas but often fail in execution. It reminds us that it is better to execute well on a few ideas than to continually generate ideas which are then subject to poor execution.

Nayar, Vineet. *Employees First, Customers Second*. Boston: Harvard Business Review Press, 2010.

    This book brilliantly challenges the notion that the customer always comes first, pointing out that, by focusing on your employees first, you are sure to provide unparalleled service to your customers.

MacKay, Harvey. *Swim With The Sharks Without Being Eaten Alive*. New York: HarperCollins Publishers, Inc., 1988.

    I love Harvey Mackay's concise style. This book is short on theory and long on practical, "how to" advice derived from real-world experience.

Lencioni, Patrick. *The Five Dysfunctions of a Team*. San Francisco: Jossey-Bass, 2002.

    I enjoy anything that Patrick Lencioni writes. I also recommend *The Three Signs of a Miserable Job: A Fable for Managers (And Their Employees)*. Lencioni understands, more than any other author, the importance of organizational health. He points out that all of the strategy in the world is worthless in a dysfunctional company.